Muthena Paul Alk author living in E lished broadly in t *Christianity* magaz his travel articles have been published in the *Independent*. His first book, *Love Changes Everything*, is published by Scripture Union, and his second, *Heart of a Hooligan*, by Highland Books.

CHRIST AND THE KALASHNIKOV

The Inspiring Story of Ian Loring as told to Muthena Paul Alkazraji

Marshall Pickering
An Imprint of HarperCollins*Publishers*

Marshall Pickering is an imprint of
HarperCollins*Religious*
part of HarperCollins*Publishers*
77–85 Fulham Palace Road, London W6 8JB
www.christian-publishing.com

First published in Great Britain in 2001
by HarperCollins*Religious*

1 3 5 7 9 10 8 6 4 2

A catalogue record for this book is available from the British Library.

ISBN 0 551 03262 6

Printed and bound in Great Britain by
Omnia Books Limited, Glasgow

CONTENTS

Acknowledgements   vii
Prologue: Bombs over Belgrade   ix

  1 'Where Is Your Treasure?'   1
  2 Midnight by the Railway Tracks   12
  3 Tourists in Tirana   27
  4 Down Home among the Gun Bunkers   44
  5 Over the Edge to Ersekë   68
  6 Mountain Pioneering   84
  7 My Queen of Armenia   100
  8 The Cross and the Kalashnikov   119
  9 Fruit Trees in the Churchyard   140
10 Sunrise over Kosova   151

Epilogue   174
Contact Details   176

ACKNOWLEDGEMENTS

The work of the Kingdom of God is invariably the privilege of a body of believers working in relationship and not the work of any individual or couple. We would like to acknowledge this by dedicating this book to some of those who have been along-side us at various times: Arthur and Brenda Thurston, who believed in us from the very beginning; Korky and Anni Davey, who encouraged and challenged us; Linda McIntrye, who believed Albania would open and lived that faith before others would even dream so; Sam and Betsy Reeves, who affirmed and encouraged us at numerous times and in numerous ways; Mike Brown, who offered wisdom and support in those hard early days; Barth and Matilda Campanjen, for being shoulders to cry on and offering vision to grasp hold of; and Mark and Ruth Stoscher, who have been the best co-workers and friends any-one could ask for. Their compassion and loyalty are an inspiration.

Ian and Caralee Loring

I would like to say *faleminderit* to: Ian and Caralee for making time to co-operate with interviews and comments; Mum and Colin for all your support; Korky Davey for first taking me 'down home among the gun bunkers'; to David Fanstone and the OAC UK National Council; to Mark and Ruth Stoscher for the gift of those crucial apartment-sitting days; to my new wife Albana for love, prayer, coffee and translation; to her family for the warmth of their welcome and *chai mali*; and to everyone who helped us begin our own first chapter together, in Albania and England, from spring through to autumn 2000.

Muthena Paul Alkazraji

PROLOGUE

Bombs over Belgrade

A Tomahawk cruise missile seared off the deck of a US warship, its brilliant glare trailing upwards through the night sky above the Adriatic Sea. Waves of jet fighter aircraft were taking off from bases in Italy on night-time sorties, and B52s were swooping down from RAF Fairford in England. Beyond the suburban lights of Belgrade, there were deep reverberating thuds and flashes of orange as fuel dumps and telecommunications systems were knocked out. Pristina, the capital of Kosova, was clothed in blackness while the air raid sirens wailed in alarm. Inside Kosova the Serbian military convoys concealed their movements as lines of smoke rose above the roofs of rural hamlets. At NATO headquarters in Brussels, the English spokesman Jamie Shea was briefing the world's media. It was the last week of March 1999, and Operation Allied Force, NATO's aerial bombardment of Serbia, was in full swing.

For many weeks now, I had been watching events around Kosova unfold on the TV screen. I was in a small town named Ersekë, close to the Greek border in the southeast of Albania and just a long day's drive from the Kosovan border crossing at Kukes. At the church that I was pastoring there, we, like everyone else in the country and around the world, were feeling deeply emotional about the escalating situation in Kosova. For months, ethnic Albanians had been fleeing over the borders of neighbouring countries. With the start of NATO's bombing campaign, thousands had begun to flood into Albania every hour, bringing with them horror stories of forced evictions and killings. The small lakeside town of Kukes had seen over a hundred thousand refugees amass around it, straining its meagre infrastructure to breaking point. The north of the country was filling up to capacity with huge overcrowded encampments. Tirana too was bursting at the seams.

At our church, a small stone house we had renovated, around a hundred believers gathered to worship. There, every Sunday, the music group would lead us in a new verse they had written to a Jewish melody. When social anarchy had swept into our town in 1997, just two years earlier, we sang, 'Lord, we pray for peace in Ersekë' with all our hearts; now we added fervently, 'Lord, we pray for peace in Kosova'. There seemed to be little more that we could do for the fleeing Kosovars, except perhaps think about making a journey up through the mountainous roads to the north to lend a hand where we could.

And then came the day that I was called to a hastily arranged meeting in Ersekë's Italianate town hall. Tiku, the mayor, a good-looking man in his thirties who habitually smoothed his side-parting tidy, welcomed me to his office. In its wall were a couple of bullet holes, and a couch sagged unevenly.

'Mirë se erdhe. Pull up a seat, Jani,' he began, gesturing towards a chair. Two other people were present: Niko, the state governor, and a man I had first met years earlier, Beni Zylyftari, the state chief of police. Beni was wearing one of his neatly pressed suits, which always looked a little stressed by his muscular physique. We all shook hands.

'A state of semi-emergency has been declared across the country,' announced Beni. 'Tirana is saying we're in danger of destabilisation in the north. They are issuing all police chiefs with extra powers.'

'The word we're getting is that, sooner or later, the government are going to want to send refugees as far south as us,' said Tiku, tapping out a slim cigarette from a white box.

'Do you really think that's likely?' I put in, surprised.

Beni nodded. 'It's looking that way.'

'How many are they talking about, Beni?' asked Niko. 'What could we do for them here?'

'We don't know what the numbers might be yet,' replied Beni. 'Maybe a couple of hundred, maybe more.'

'If it came to it, where could we put them?' Tiku chipped in. 'Could the church help again?'

I thought about it briefly. 'We'll do what we can,' I replied. 'There's room at the upper kindergarten for people, but there's nothing in there – just cold stone floors. What about down at the school dormitory?'

Our conversation continued for a while as we all considered what seemed a matter of theoretical speculation. It seemed improbable – Ersekë was just too far south.

About a week later, as I lay on our settee dozing in front of the silent TV screen, the telephone rang. I fumbled for the receiver.

'*Allo. Kush je?*'

'*Allo,* Jani? *Jam* Beni! Can you come over to the police station?'

'Can't it wait, Beni? It's after 10.30!'

'I've been sent down some forms from the Interior Ministry. They want an assessment of how many refugees Ersekë can cope with, and they want it tonight!'

'Oh, I see,' I replied. I sat up, a little reluctantly, and drank my cold black coffee.

Late that evening, Beni, Tiku, Niko and I set off together to scout around the town. The street-lights in the square buzzed noisily as we passed under them, and the apartment blocks were lit with chequerboards of red and white windows. I remember a single tyre blazing on a corner. Above us the stars were clear above our corner of the Balkans, and the night air was bracing as we trudged over the remaining patches of snow. We walked around the town's old kindergarten building, and around the new one that the church had been renovating. We looked at disused factory buildings with shattered windows and broken roofs – anywhere we could think of – counting up a rough tally of how many people each location might take. Later in the night, as I slept, Beni had our estimate for two and a half thousand refugees dispatched back to Tirana. Ersekë itself was home to just seven thousand people. If such a number ever came here, I reflected, the influx would be almost overwhelming.

In the early hours of the morning two days later, I heard the frantic honking of a car horn outside our apartment block. It sounded like an alarm inside my head. I pulled aside the bed sheets and stumbled my way through to the living-room window. Below me in the lane, headlights were glaring in the darkness, and I could just make out the shape of Beni's Mercedes. Moments later, there was a hammering on the door. In the stairwell stood Beni's chauffeur, breathing heavily. 'Quickly, quickly,' he shouted. 'They are coming, Jani! They are coming! The refugees will be here in a couple of hours.'

As I made my way through the town, picking my way round the dark, icy puddles, the questions I'd been building up for weeks began to turn over in my thoughts. I had agreed with Tiku and Beni that the church could act as a staging post, but how much of the responsibility in the town might fall on our shoulders after that? And for how many? I had seen the horror in the Kosovars' eyes as they had pointed back along the road to Prizren in front of the waiting news crews at Kukes. What kind of condition would they be in? And how long would they remain here with us? They would need food, clothing and bedding, not to mention psychological support, and we didn't have any material provisions for them. How on earth would we cope? The Lord had taken us to the edge so many times before; but I wondered where he would lead us now. As the church had prayed for the Kosovars, many of us had felt touched by the spirit of Matthew 25: 'Whatever you do for one of the least of these brothers of mine, you do for me.' Up ahead, the lights of the church were on. I felt a strengthening determination to serve, to do everything in my power for them, and for the Lord, with his strength.

1 'WHERE IS YOUR TREASURE?'

Such a spirit of compassion and service had not always guided my heart. In fact, for many years before my arrival in Albania, my principal ambition in life had been to make myself as wealthy and successful as my business ideas and opportunities would let me. I had set about achieving this goal with a hard-nosed determination that at times used and sacrificed others as a means to that sole end. It had always seemed far more important to me to succeed than to care for people. At secondary school I had set the bar in my life at achieving my first million by the age of 30, and that was what I had tried to do. But that was before one evening in Bristol, England, a decade earlier, when, as I sat in the bath until the water had long turned cold, everything that I had been trying to make of myself was made inescapably clear to me by the Lord.

For most of my comfortable childhood in the sixties and seventies, I was raised in a middle-class environment in the pleasant rural area of the Chew Valley, just south of the city of Bristol. I have no idea how much it subconsciously affected my view of God, but I remember as a young boy feeling cheated by a local vicar out of a payment for singing in the choir. As it was, somewhere around the age of 12, I moved from being agnostic to feeling positively atheistic in my view of life and its meaning. I had decided firmly that I did not believe in God: for me, it was life and then nothing, evolution and very probably the 'big bang'. As I grew older, these issues became matters I would regularly debate with others who I knew professed faith in Christ, sometimes when they raised the subject of God themselves and sometimes when I goaded them into an argument with me. I remember turning red with fury when I felt pushed into an intellectual corner; more often, however, I would feel that I had the upper hand. At secondary school I hated Religious Education classes, and my assessment of the Christians I met was never a particularly glowing one. To me they seemed to exist in a ghetto, holding their Christian Union meetings once a week and going about their activities with at best a maintenance mentality and more often an attitude of retreat. They were, I felt, never the movers and the shakers. Later, at university, my negative views were further reinforced by the number of Christians who wanted to engage in debate based entirely on a book that they provided. If it came to debating the existence of 'a' god, fine, I felt, we could do it. But nine times out of ten their argument seemed to require a huge empty leap of faith that Christ was God because their Bible said so. In that, for me, even the best of the debaters lost their credibility.

By the time it came to making educational choices for my future, I had decided that what I wanted out of life was material wealth and success, and that the place where you got that was plainly the business world. My father had run a successful carpet business through most of my formative years, and these were the things that he valued himself; perhaps, to a degree, my choice was influenced by a desire for his approval. At the technical college in the nearby seaside town of Weston-super-Mare, I chose to study 'A' levels in Law, Economics and Business Studies, and my grades were high enough to allow me to carry on to university.

For most of my twenties I worked for a successful retail and finance corporation at various locations along the M4 corridor from Bristol to London. The corporation owned every kind of enterprise from toy stores to manufacturing businesses, and it was also in the regular process of acquiring more, stripping them down and selling them off. The first time I was used by the organization for such an assignment was when I had to handle the take-over of a whole group of – ironically – carpet and furniture shops in mid-Wales. I had seen take-overs happening on paper in our offices many times before, but to be the man who carried it out on the front-line was an uncomfortable shock. Among other tasks, I had to fire all the chain's employees and give credible reasons to each of them. The cold business reality was that their assets could be used in a different way to make more profit. Though I felt a little sadness that their livelihoods were coming to an end, I felt frustration with them, too.

Later it fell to me to fire fifty people in four days. Such people never made my job easy. 'Can't they see that if their company isn't performing, the writing's on the wall? Why swim against the tide?' I reasoned with myself. Initially, I felt a level of unease about the world I was involved in, but somewhere along the way I crossed over a line and became part of it. My outlook seemed to harden as I breathed in the environment. What was most important to me was to go the next leg along my own motor-way to personal wealth, and I came to a place of having no compunction about dumping someone else along the business hard-shoulder to get there. At times I even planned the location to do it. I wanted money: it was that simple. And as is the way in much of the modern business world, the lines of what was right and wrong became very grey at times. So it was, at the age of 27, after pursuing one goal since I'd dreamt it up at secondary school and coming closer than I had ever been to achieving it, that I flunked in a major way. Through a series of bad decisions, both professional and moral, the whole conveyance of my life careered off the road and crashed.

One afternoon in the spring of 1990, as I walked through the precincts of Bristol's Broadmead shopping centre, I noticed a small crowd gathered to one side of a travel agent's window. At the front of the huddle stood a man painting letters on to what looked like a large artist's easel. Out of passing curiosity, I joined the rear of the crowd. The man, an ageing Irishman with a ruddy nose, broke into song, and seemed to have a quality of almost carefree joy about him that was so far from my own emotional state.

'I was a drunk-en al-co-ho-lic bum,' he announced, with a bouncing lilt in his voice. 'But he took me from the mire and he put me into the choir!'

I caught on pretty quickly that he was making some form of Christian presentation, and I turned on my heel and walked on, feeling I wanted to spit on the ground. 'What a right load of blooming codswallop,' I thought. But I was curious to see what he would do with his easel and to hear the end of his talk. After a moment I returned and stood closer, with my intellect loaded like a rifle with all the refutations I had cultivated and polished through school and university.

The Irishman presented the Christian message: how the world was God's and how the basic problem with humanity was its sinfulness; how God had become human in Jesus Christ, taken the punishment we deserved for our wrongdoing, and shone as a light, then and now, into human life. The talk and the way he had used his easel held me, but I remained unmoved and unconvinced by its substance. As the crowd broke up someone tried to engage me in conversation, but I brushed past and made my way along the shop fronts.

It was two months later, early one evening, as I tried to ease the sting of my circumstances in the comfort of a long bath, that I saw myself with a new, painful clarity. I put my book down on the tub's rim, and lowered my head under the water.

All was silent but for the faint sounds of the tap dripping near my feet. For a moment I felt fully shrouded in warmth, and that was consolation of a kind. Psychologically, the death of my ambitions had left me feeling as if I had driven into the concrete pillars of a motorway bridge. I felt buckled up, without any destination or real desire for one. I let myself float back up to the surface and pushed my hair back from my forehead. My eyes focussed on the rising steam and the ripples from the tap as they rode slowly over the surface to my nose.

Then I heard someone speaking to me. I could see no one, and I couldn't locate the voice in any one place in the room. I slid up to a sitting position, the water running down my arms and chest. Goose bumps rose across my skin.

The voice had a gentle authority: 'Do not store up for yourself treasure on earth where moth and rust destroy. But store up for yourself treasure in heaven. For where your treasure is, there your heart will be also.

'No one can serve two masters. Either he will hate the one and love the other, or he will be devoted to the one and despise the other. You cannot serve both God and Money.'

I looked around to see if I was still in a bathtub, but the words cut me instantly to the bone. I knew that this was God. God had chosen to speak to me, and I was silenced by it. I saw myself with a sudden irrefutable clarity. I knew what had held mastery over my years, and who it was that I had hated. I saw again the drive that I'd had for personal profit and the arguments I'd used to goad others. I ran my hands down my face to wipe clear the scummy water. Slowly a heavy grief came over me, and I shook with it as I sat there and wept. I began to speak to the voice as if God was in the room with me. There were relationships and situations that I felt shame about, things I felt I wanted to open out to his view. It was as if some organ of con-

5

science had pulsed with new life again. I wept further as I explained things in a low voice.

'I didn't believe who you were,' I said. 'I didn't believe it. But if you are who you are, how can I not serve you now?'

It must have been over an hour later that I stood up in the cold bathwater. I had a mind to find a copy of the Bible and to read the words that I had heard.

From the evening that God revealed himself to me, I developed an insatiable appetite for reading the Bible. I read page after page and book after book, carrying it with me everywhere I went. I had read it in its entirety within a week, and I returned to verses and books again and again. For the next six months I felt guilty about reading anything else, even a newspaper, and I rarely did so. With the passages that I struggled to understand – and I came to them daily – I would pray to God, 'Lord, help me to grasp this, as if I were there with you at the time!' Frequently it would seem that my prayers were answered directly. At night, in that drowsy state that immediately precedes sleep, I would drift into dream-like visions of biblical stories that would bring the Bible to vivid life for me. Sometimes it felt as if I were reading the book all day and dreaming it all night.

As for prayer, the only previous experience I'd had of it was listening to the formal public intercessions at the primary school I attended. Now I found I was able to talk to God in conversation, as if he were a friend and father who knew me well and took me just as I was.

On one occasion, as I walked by the docks in the centre of Bristol, I was struck afresh by the beauty of a tree growing close to the water's edge. I sat on a bench and stared at it. The leaves were rustling in the sunlight, and as my eyes followed leaf to twig, twig to branch, and branch to the trunk, I realized how my life had closed me down to the beauty around me. Now it seemed that suddenly I could see so many things with fresh eyes.

Because of the intensity of my experiences, I seriously began to doubt whether many other people had personal relationships with God at all. I visited a number of churches in the city, hoping to find other believers who felt as I now did about the Lord, but they reminded me of all my worst memories of church from childhood. There were very few people there, and all of them looked dour and sat safe distances apart on the pews. I began to wonder whatever had happened to the church and how many other believers were actually living in these times. I wondered if I might be one of the very few in existence, and these thoughts were deeply troubling.

A couple of days after I had been to a particularly depressing service I decided to telephone a man whose name had been given to me by an acquaintance. The man ministered at a Brethren assembly, and as we spoke he invited me to a service at Speedwell Gospel Hall, a simply decorated chapel on the east side of the city, followed by lunch at his house. That Sunday, the congregation there struck me immediately: they may have seemed a little old-fashioned, but they were clearly genuine in their love of each other and God – and I was touched by it. My host, Arthur Thurston, was a plain-speaking Cockney who limped with the bearing of an ex-serviceman. Back at his house, he and his wife Brenda made me feel warmly welcome, and in Arthur's company I felt that I had found someone I could truly open up to. During the afternoon I told Arthur everything: about my life in the business world, about the intensity of my experience in the bathtub, and about my fears that I might be one of the few believers alive. Arthur listened patiently.

'What do you think? Am I crazy?' I enquired tentatively as I finished.

'It's a wonderful thing that the Lord has revealed himself to you in such a way, Ian, and I praise him for it. But if you think

7

that he's working only in your life, you're suffering from a heavy dose of pride and arrogance, son,' he replied curtly.

I felt squarely brought down to earth, but I was also relieved.

'Now,' he continued, pushing his glasses up the bridge of his nose, 'do you know that the Lord saves people for a purpose? So when are you going to get up off your rear end and start helping him?'

I sank a little lower into my seat. I knew that I had served myself as long as I had been a working adult, but when I'd heard the Lord's voice I had truly chosen to turn all my working energies his way.

'I want to serve, Arthur. I believe I have been called to, but I really don't know where to begin,' I explained. 'How do you do it?'

'You need to get equipped, Ian,' he replied. 'Now, there's someone coming here for tea today who might be able to help you with that. Why don't you hang around?'

Later that afternoon I met Arthur's friend. The man worked with an evangelistic agency called Open Air Campaigners, and he was heading up a school for the training of evangelists in the city.

'Why don't you come along and see how it goes? Take it a step at a time, and God will show you the right way forward,' he suggested. A door had opened right in front of me.

The following Monday morning, feeling a little like a fresher without any A-levels in my subject, I began attending the Bristol School of Evangelism at St Philip's and St Jacob's, a traditional Anglican church in the centre of the city. Along with sixteen other students, I sat through the school's seminars on theology, apologetics, preaching theory and evangelistic approaches and methods, including using an easel – or sketchboard, as they called it – like the one I had seen the red-nosed

Irishman use outside the travel agent's window. In the afternoons we did practical work in schools, on the streets and
door-to-door to consolidate all that we were learning. The
breadth of our training was to be extensive. For me, it was the
start of an intense phase of learning, and with it coming so
soon after the Lord had revealed himself to me in the tub, I felt
I was trying to catch up on a huge amount of ground simply
to draw level with my fellow students. I often wondered how
gifted I was for the calling I was preparing myself for.

After classes, I regularly spent my evenings with Arthur and
Brenda, where I was always welcomed with tea and toast and
warm encouragement in the faith. They became like second
parents to me. All the while, my appetite for the Bible remained
voracious, and through the intensity of all that I was learning
and the deepening awareness of the person I had once been, it
seemed that God was breaking my heart and remaking me.

As Christmas approached and the dark Bristol evenings crept
back into the afternoons, all trainees at the school were encouraged to begin praying about their futures. What was discon-
certing for me was that most students already seemed to have
a clear idea of where they were heading. I prayed, but I didn't
have a clue. I asked God for guidance, but I felt I might as well
be shouting out loud in a soundproof booth. Had I been heard
or not? Where was the reply?

On one of those evenings, a course tutor by the name of
Korky, a pukka yachtsman of a character with a silver beard,
asked me and another student if we would show two visiting
Bulgarian pastors around some of the West Country's tourist
attractions. As Tom and I sat with them in Bath's magnificent
golden-stone abbey, our relationship with the two pastors
deepened. One of the men began to express his distress about
the social conditions in his country and the struggles of his
church since Communism had crumbled. Beneath the high

stained-glass windows, we all cried and prayed as they told us stories that made their country's massive food shortages and widespread hunger seem all the more heart-rending.

I could see the way Tom's mind was working from the expression in his eyes as we left. 'The church here ought to be able to do something to help them,' he whispered. I felt exactly the same.

That night I felt a growing conviction that God was tapping me on the shoulder about Bulgaria, but I tried to brush the feeling aside. For the next two days I felt an uneasy guilt, and then on the third day the conviction grew steadily again. As I lay in bed late that evening, drifting towards the edge of sleep, I sensed God speaking to me quietly in my spirit.

'So are you going to do it? You keep praying about what to do next, and I've told you. It's three days later, and you still haven't started. Are you going to do it?'

I sat up straight. I lifted aside the bed covers and swung my legs down on to the floor. My heart was beating quickly.

Now it became a passion in me to ensure that we brought help out from the churches in Bristol to the churches of Bulgaria's capital, Sofia. Over the first few months of 1991, I spoke wherever Arthur and others would introduce me to congregations, raising money. Open Air Campaigners put word out in their prayer letters, and soon a critical mass of funds had been reached. I found drivers and trucks, organized documentation, and arranged for the purchase of basic foodstuffs, medical supplies and copies of the Gospels. I was running on a huge surge of adrenaline.

Early in the spring, I rode out to the Balkans with Bob Atkin, a lorry driver with a rich West Country accent, delivering the aid shipment. In April we drove back to Sofia on a further aid and evangelism mission, taking with us some of my fellow students at the school, including Caralee, a petite Californian with dark, curly hair.

We drove down the main highway into Greece to the port city of Thessaloniki. Here we were to buy more aid for our lorry to transport back up to Sofia, and we took advantage of the stop to rest for a few weeks. One evening, Linda, an English missionary who was our contact there, made a request for a little help with her work.

'There are groups of Albanians, illegals, hiding out in some of the railway yards here now. I'd like to visit them, but the best time is at night. The darkness gives them a little protection,' she explained, speaking in her characteristic rapid sentences. 'I don't want to go alone. Would you come along with me?'

We all had time on our hands and we were game to help out. Little did we realize that Linda's invitation was to be the prelude to a series of dramatic events we could never have anticipated.

2 MIDNIGHT BY THE RAILWAY TRACKS

I felt a little apprehensive when, late one evening, we followed
Linda into a railway carriage dump yard. The night sky above
Thessaloniki was tinged with the white glow of the city's street-
lights, and the outlines of freight wagons that had once trun-
dled the lines of northern Greece rose up close by in long dark
lines. The air smelt of diesel and refuse and the gravel crunched
noisily under our feet, making our approach obvious to anyone
hiding hereabouts. Some distance ahead of us, I noticed a small
cluster of flames flickering amongst the bushes.

'Ssshhh. Over there – I think there's someone,' I whispered to
the others.

'Let's be cautious, Ian,' Caralee whispered back, tugging at
the edge of my shirt to restrain me.

We stepped across the tracks, instinctively glancing both
ways, and then walked together slowly along the hard dirt verge
towards the flames. Before us I could soon make out the half-
lit faces of a group of men watching us; nearby, I could see the
silhouettes of others bedding down at the edge of the tracks.
Some of them stirred from beneath stiff sections of covering
and sat up. One man gathered his belongings and scuttled away
under a carriage.

'Er … It's okay,' I called out, hoping that one of them might
understand English. 'We're not police … We have some chicken

and some juice for you.' One man jumped to his feet and turned to face us; there was a certain confidence in his bearing.

I walked a little closer and offered my hand. 'My name is Ian,' I said.

Linda stepped forward, peering through her heavy-framed glasses, and introduced our group. '*Unë jam* Linda. *Kjo është* Caralee *dhe* Bob.'

For a moment the man studied us, and then he whispered a couple of words to the rest of the men. He took a couple of paces forward. 'Nikos,' he replied, placing his palm on his chest.

Linda took out some cartons of juice and passed them to me. Nikos beckoned us forward, and I sat down on the ground close to the edge of the tracks.

'Where have you come from?' Linda asked him.

'We are all Albanians here. These are some of my men,' Nikos said, pointing around at the rest of his group, who all regarded us cautiously in the firelight. 'We were stationed in the mountains … on the border at Qafë e Kazanit. Our duty was to prevent others from leaving our country. Everything is breaking down there now; everything is changing … Two weeks ago, they said to me, "Nikos, we are leaving. There is nothing in our country," and they began to take off their uniforms.'

The other men were now nodding their agreement. Nikos continued: 'I said to them, "Put your uniforms back on or I will shoot you!" They said, "You can shoot us. There is nothing here. Communism is finished, Nikos." I took my gun and I pointed it at them. I said, "Don't make me do it!" But I couldn't do it. How could I? So I took off my uniform and I came with them.'

Our group sat with theirs for a while, and we talked about the situation in their home country and passed around the cartons of juice until I sensed the moment had arrived to take things further. 'Nikos, we have come here to tell you and your

13

men about the God of Heaven and Earth who loves all peoples,' I began, and Linda translated. The men listened with their eyes widening, but after a couple of minutes Linda glanced back at me as the right words evaded her.

'I just don't have enough of the language yet,' she sighed.

'Let's pray,' I said. 'Lord, thank you for Linda and for the Albanian she has learnt, but you know what it is you want to say to them. Just as you did for Joseph and Daniel, speak to them in visions and dreams.'

Linda took out a stack of copies of Luke's Gospel from a plastic bag and put them down on the gravel. We handed them to Nikos and his men, and to others who had gathered around. I looked at my watch; it was gone midnight. We shook hands with the men and said that we would come again the next night if they would like us to. Nikos nodded graciously.

Late the following evening we made our way along the tracks towards the railway carriages once more. Ahead of us, the flames of the fire drew us towards the Albanians. A large group had gathered and were talking and gesturing to each other excitedly. When Nikos saw us coming, he strode over to meet us with a look of wonder in his eyes. He seemed radiant. His men pointed towards us as we approached.

Nikos began to talk rapidly to Linda and she translated. 'Last night, Jani, I read your book to my men. I told them that it was important for them to listen. In the morning when I awoke, they were looking at me. No one was saying anything! Their faces were different. I said to them, "You all saw him too, didn't you?"'

The men were quietly saying, 'Po ... Po.'

Nikos continued: 'Last night, he stood here by the fire. His clothes were white and clean. He said to us, "You are my sheep, and I am your shepherd. Come to me ..." and he held out his hands.'

I looked around at Caralee. I was choked up. When we had said the prayer, we had hardly believed it would be answered in such a way.

A tall man in the group now emptied out his sack of possessions on to the ground: some clothes and a newspaper tumbled out, and a plate followed with a clatter. He gestured to Linda that he wanted to fill the sack with copies of the Gospel, and as she handed over those she had with her he heaped them in excitedly. We saw this man just once more, the following day. We learnt then that he had been passing the Gospels out to other Albanians near the city's university. After that, he swung all that he had left over his shoulder and left directly for Albania, such was his desire to share immediately all that he had discovered.

It was April 1991, and after more than forty years of dominance and control over the lives of its people, Albania's Communist government was beginning to lose some of its total grip on power. Only a few weeks earlier, the first fugitives had begun to traverse the high mountain ridges in the northwest of Greece until they stumbled across the railway tracks. They followed the lines southeastwards through the countryside, finally reaching the cities. Here they were hiding from the authorities, almost frozen with the culture shock of having arrived in 'the West' and at a loss as to what exactly they should do next.

From the night we discovered Nikos and his men sheltering beneath the railway wagons, it seemed that something had been set in motion. We met them again regularly, and as we talked they would explain with amazement how one of their group had prayed for a new pair of shoes and been given them, or how another had asked the Lord for food to eat and a passer-by had subsequently invited them into a café and footed the bill. Their simple prayers were being answered on a daily basis, and we, like them, were in awe at the outpouring of God's grace.

Nikos and his men quickly began to introduce us to other Albanians they had befriended in the railway yards, and they too were eager to receive the message and blessings of God's saving love. The soldiers themselves became committed evangelists. Later, as the refugees became bolder, we met them in the city centre, below the concrete apartment buildings that rose block after block up to the old town, and at the beach as the freight ships and white liners passed out at sea. We would pray with them, asking the Lord to reveal himself in his own way to those who were ready to receive, and then hand out our copies of Luke's Gospel. Sometimes the meetings would dissolve in an instant if a refugee spotted the Greek police. One minute a crowd would be gathered around us excitedly, the next they would be scattering towards the trees or side streets for cover. They knew that the treatment they would receive if they were caught would hardly be sympathetic.

When just Caralee and I met up with the refugees, we would attempt to communicate by picking out single words from a copy of an English–Albanian dictionary, stripped of all religious phrases by its Communist publishers. Though it sometimes took us up to three hours to make a simple presentation of God's desire that they should return to him, time and time again he seemed to lead us, and the right word would leap out of the page: Perëndia – God; njeriu – man; mashtrim – deception. The refugees listened attentively, their heads tilted on one side.

For the next four weeks it seemed that we would bump into Albanians wherever we were in Thessaloniki. Some of the churches in the city began opening up kitchens to feed the many who were coming to faith, and Linda made a quiet arrangement with a couple of Christian restaurateurs to feed any refugees who turned up with a special 'free meal' voucher. It was risky for the owners to feed the illegals, and also for the Albanians to be seen in public places, but the Lord worked it discreetly to good effect.

Throughout it all, I had a growing feeling of destiny. Somehow, I and those who were working with us in Thessaloniki were in exactly the right place at the right time, and I was buzzing with the exhilaration of it all. God was doing something very special among the Albanians in the city: so many were coming to faith and experiencing real answers to their prayers. I remember one man's stubble-covered face beaming as he tossed his cigarettes into the air and then stamped all over them on the pavement. 'I won't smoke another one of these,' he pronounced. 'What I have found now is better.'

Some of the refugees went back to Albania, risking everything immediately. I had never witnessed anything like it. What we had shared with them was more valuable than everything they had risked and hoped for in Greece. They gathered up their few possessions and a handful of gospel booklets, set off back along the edge of the railway tracks towards the mountains, and were gone.

Our stay in Thessaloniki came to an end in mid-May. We left Caralee with some friends there, and Bob and I returned to Sofia to continue the remainder of our mission before setting off back for Bristol. As we sped home along the Yugoslavian autoroutes, I watched the scenery in silence. The petrol queues in Bosnia were growing and I could feel the tension in the air, but I felt little desire to return to my home city. I had been praying throughout the spring that God would reveal the next step in my life, and now my thoughts were constantly with Nikos and the other Albanian refugees.

On my first Sunday back in Bristol, after the service at Speedwell Gospel Hall I prayed with a small group of friends over afternoon tea at Arthur's house. I told them all about the men under the railway carriages, how God seemed to be doing a special work in Thessaloniki, and that this was where I felt I wanted to be.

'How's the money holding up, son?' boomed Arthur.

'I'm pretty well skint,' I said, feeling a little foolish. 'I don't know what the future will hold, Arthur, but I know where God has been using me.'

By the time the Bakewell slices were cleared away, they had placed enough money on the dining table for an air ticket.

'Get yourself back there,' said Arthur, 'and trust in the Lord for the rest.'

Within a week of arriving back in England, I was preparing to return to Greece's second city. The speed of it all was breakneck, but I had no lack of conviction for it.

On the flight from Bristol Airport back down to Thessaloniki, I sat by the window looking out at the patches of cloud and the patterns on the land way below. I thought about the man who had emptied his sack on to the road and headed off back to his country, and the faces of those who'd gathered around us as we flicked through the pages of the dictionary. I wondered where they were now – and where Caralee was, too.

Towards the end of the flight the intercom cracked on. 'Ladies and gentlemen,' began the captain. He paused for a moment. 'If you look out of the aircraft now, we are flying at an altitude of around 29,000 feet over Albania ... perhaps the most isolated of all countries under Communist rule. For almost forty years it was dominated by one dictator, Enver Hoxha. However, even in Albania the winds of change are blowing ...'

As the captain continued his résumé, I looked down towards two distant lakes, white with the light of the sun, and I felt an upwelling of peacefulness. I realized how tense I had been, and yet here, above Albania, the tension was easing. It was the same sensation I had felt working with the refugees, only more complete.

The aircraft was soon over the mountains bordering Greece, their passes now threaded with lines of Albanians hoping for a new beginning, and shortly we began to descend.

Back in Thessaloniki, Linda had been busy. She had made an important new contact, a travel agent who ran short excursions over the border to Albania, principally for Greek pro-Communists. A team of Christians was now being assembled to venture inside, with the aim of making contact with some of the refugees and their families in the southeast provincial market town of Korçë. It was a journey not without risks – very few Westerners were allowed inside Albania – but it would prove a test of what might now, for the first time, be possible there. I knew that my place was on that bus.

Early on a May morning, only two days after I had arrived back in the city, I boarded the coach with Caralee and Mike Brown, a missionary with curly blond hair. We were booked on a three-day excursion, together with two small teams from OM and YWAM and a handful of other Christian workers. Our fellow travellers, largely middle-aged Greek men, eyed our party with reserve, a little suspicious of this sudden show of solidarity from their Western comrades.

The large blue and white coach was around three-quarters full and the air-conditioning was broken, so I figured the journey was going to get sticky. As the coach accelerated out through the suburbs and past the rows of hoardings advertising cigarettes, I glanced around at other members of our party. I could sense both excitement and apprehension in their eyes. I felt the same way too. We had decided that in addition to contacting refugees in Korçë, we were going to test just what else we could get away with.

Three hours later, our coach began to climb into the mountainous border region, the road snaking for mile after mile high above the town of Florina way below us on the hazy plain. All along the route we were praying – praying that God would lead and preserve us. 'Lord, please guard all the members of our party with your loving attention, and open up the doors of opportunity for your kingdom,' I whispered, with my hand partially concealing my face.

Soon the road deteriorated to a rough-surfaced dirt track barely wide enough for the coach to navigate. We pressed our faces to the window and instinctively pulled away as the trees brushed past. There had never been a flow of cross-border traffic here, and the route had seen few motor vehicles since World War II.

The border checkpoint on the Albanian side was a wooden sentry box with the paint peeling off it and a rusty chain stretching across the road to a pole. The handful of soldiers standing guard looked demoralized in their rough-woven green uniforms tipped with red insignia on the collars. As our passports were stamped with 'Kapshtice', the name of the crossing, three Albanians boarded the coach: two men wearing identical brown suit jackets, and a woman who introduced herself as a translator. I surmised that they must be Sigurimi, employees of the Albanian secret police, sent to keep a close eye on the whole coach party. As the bus rolled past the sentry box, I looked down at a young soldier: he averted his eyes, seemingly in fear.

We entered the first few metres of Albania and it dawned on me that we were here. I felt my heartbeat quicken, and yet I had an even deeper sense of the peace I had felt on the aeroplane. It was not a simple absence of fear, but a tangible presence of something. I looked back at Caralee; she smiled and opened her eyes wider in a knowing expression.

I'd had vague ideas of how the country might appear, but in truth I was uncertain of what to expect. As we rolled down the pass, following the course of a stream, and came to the first village, all our faces were pressed to the windows. I'd heard about the machine-gun bunkers built to fortify the country against the world outside, but the sheer quantity was astonishing. They covered the landscape in all directions like clusters of mushrooms after rain. Stationed around the hills were numerous artillery positions with gun-barrels nosing out in readiness. The slogans of governance were everywhere: on the hillsides, laid out in white stones by prisoners, and painted on the sides of buildings in Soviet-style script, they read, 'Glory to the 23rd Congress', 'Glory to the Party', 'Glory to Enver.' People we passed at the roadside were dressed in drab colours, either brown, green or grey and nothing more, and like the soldiers they seemed to avoid our gaze, looking away at some nearby spot of ground. There were only donkeys and mule-drawn carts on the road, yet all along each side, mile after mile, I noticed a line of magnificent silver birches swaying in the late spring breeze.

As the coach drew into the outskirts of Korçë, two young men began running alongside, waving and shouting. I recognized them from the parks in Thessaloniki as Alban and Sokoli. They had noticed the coach pulling in, and were overjoyed to spot us on board. When finally we stepped off the coach outside the concrete monolith of the Hotel Iliria, I shook hands with them and indicated quickly that we would meet them later.

Our coach party was chaperoned briskly into the hotel. For the remainder of the afternoon we toured the scheduled sites in Korçë, waiting for the free time when we could meet up with Sokoli and make contact with others. I remember being shown a few relics of an Orthodox church as evidence that not all traces of religious practice had been destroyed in the country, but it was clear that by and large there was little left.

That evening, our group assembled in the hotel restaurant. Outside, crowds pressed their faces to the windows, watching our food being served. As grace was said, away from the eyes of the Sigurimi, I felt little real gratitude for the meal: a bowl of thin meat soup covered with a layer of oil. But then it came to me that those on the other side of the glass would have eaten it without hesitation. There was real hunger out there.

At the entrance to a park behind the hotel, away from the street-lights, Caralee and I met Sokoli, a wily young lad with blond hair, and a small group of other refugees. Sokoli shook his head in disbelief that we had come.

'Jani, Jani, *jeni ju*,' he grinned.

With the little Albanian I had, I explained our party's plan. 'Sokoli … tomorrow … here … 4 p.m. … a talk … get the word out … tell all your friends and families … okay?'

He nodded. We shook hands quickly and said goodbye. The Albanians slipped stealthily away across the grass; speaking to foreigners still ran the risk of punishment.

The itinerary for the next afternoon was a visit to a further Orthodox site at the nearby town of Voskopoje, but we had no intention of going. When the time for departure came, the entire team feigned illness. I shrugged my shoulders and pointed to my stomach. The security service men eyed us with frustration, but there was little they could do about it. One of them was obliged to leave with the translator and the Greeks. Later that afternoon, as we hovered around the hotel lobby anxiously biding our time, I sensed that there were many others in the building watching us.

At a quarter to four I glanced round at the team. It was time to step out, and my stomach seemed to rise as if speeding across a hump-backed bridge in a car. Together we walked through the glass entrance doors and around to the park at the rear. The security officer scurried quickly after us. As we crossed the grass my heart sank; there were scarcely more than thirty people ahead, casting their eyes around uneasily, and I couldn't see Sokoli. I wondered whether our plan was really of the Holy Spirit, or just foolhardy. We quickly set up a sketch-board to paint a visual message, and the YWAM team began to perform a short drama.

It was then that I noticed something. All around the edge of the park, people were watching at a distance. As the presentation continued they began to edge timidly forward, glancing at each other and at us. By the time the drama drew to a close, we were surrounded by literally hundreds of people.

The moment had arrived to preach a short message, and yet no one spoke Albanian fluently enough to do it. I glanced around anxiously, grasping my Bible, and then began in English.

Suddenly a young man with curly brown hair stepped out of the crowd. 'My name is Ardian,' he said quickly. 'I will translate for you.'

As I continued to speak, Ardian relayed the message confidently to the crowd. My pulse was racing. I was amazed and I thanked God under my breath. As I spoke, I watched the faces of those in front of us as they jostled and craned their necks for a better view. I had never witnessed a crowd polarize so visibly to what they were hearing: an ageing woman in a black head-scarf, whose eyes narrowed as she pulled away; a teenage boy with a half-grown moustache, whose mouth began to widen like a fish. It was as if a light was shining so clearly in the park that there were no grey areas, just highlight and shadow across the people's faces.

When Ardian finished translating, he concluded, as if his heart had made its own choice as he'd stood there: 'I know this message is true, because it was so for me.'

I stepped up on to the edge of a small stone platform. By now the crowd had spread back across the grass. People were climbing up trees and standing on the tops of park benches, and around the edges of the grass were dozens of soldiers who had been listening in to the talk. Suddenly, shouting broke out at the rear of the crowd and people began to scatter. Four police cars had braked in the road, and the officers seemed to be arguing among themselves as well as trying to break through the people. The soldiers, however, were crowding up to them, redfaced, pushing them back and waving their arms in the air. I looked back down at the team. It seemed like the right moment to leave. We packed up the equipment we had brought and mingled in with the crowds as the park rapidly began to empty.

Back at the hotel, we were floating but afraid. No one could quite believe the response we'd had, nor how Ardian, whom I now remembered meeting briefly in Thessaloniki, had stepped forward publicly at great risk to himself. One black mark in your biography file could mean interrogations or worse, and the Sigurimi were always watching. Our brown-suited spy had seen it all, and we knew he'd make his reports. We held our breath and waited for the ensuing consequences throughout the evening.

A soft tapping came on the door of my hotel room at around midnight. My room-mate looked anxiously across. I pulled on my shoes and moments later turned the key in the lock, opening the door cautiously.

Outside in the corridor stood an old man with dark bushy eyebrows and a warm expression. He held out his hand. 'I am Ligor Çina, a member of the church in Korçë,' he whispered, and beckoned for us to follow him. I felt a little apprehensive but at peace somehow that the man's introduction was genuine. We locked the room and followed a couple of paces behind him down the silent hotel corridor.

Just five minutes' walk from the entrance of the Hotel Iliria, we entered a small stone cottage, ducking to avoid the lintel.

The interior was dimly lit and smelt a little of feet. Ligor gestured us through a further doorway where another elderly man with dark sparkling eyes sat regally on a wooden chair, his face half-lit by a single light bulb. A candle was flickering on the window ledge. Ligor introduced the man as Koci Treska.

I stepped forward and shook his hand. Once we had sat down opposite him, he wasted no time in addressing us and I waited for my room-mate to translate. His manner seemed formal, yet I could see tears in his eyes and he brushed his cheek intermittently with his hand. Despite his frail physique, the man possessed a noticeable inner strength, and I could feel my own tears welling up before I knew what he was saying.

My room-mate turned to look at me. 'He says that he, Ligor and a handful of others are the only remaining members of a church started before the outbreak of the Second World War by two American missionaries, Kennedy and Jaques. They were the youth group,' he said, pausing while he too steadied his voice.

'He says that they have kept their faith secretly for over fifty years, and word reached him today that the gospel had been preached on the streets of his town for the first time since the Communists took control. He wanted to meet us and to thank us. He has been praying for this day for years. He says that he is ready now to die with contentment.'

Now it was my turn to brush my cheek. The old man reached forward, and for a couple of seconds we clasped hands. My room-mate continued: 'He says that we should go now, but he hopes that we will return here.' I was overcome – a lifetime of covert belief, and we were his first confidants.

Koci now gestured towards the door. The meeting was over. As we stood up to leave, Ligor stepped ahead of us. Outside the cottage, he looked both ways. We shook hands firmly and scurried away along the dark side street.

In the early morning light outside the hotel, we hugged the refugees who had come to see our party off more publicly than they or we would have dared just 72 hours before. As I watched the lines of birches and the gun-bunkers slide past along the border road, I knew that I wanted to get back inside Albania as fast as was conceivably possible. The Greeks gave us cold glances and the translator let us know that she was upset, but we made sure to stay on the right side of the coach driver when we stopped at a roadside restaurant just over the mountains. Our intention now was to let other Christian groups back in Thessaloniki know that we had discovered surviving members of the Protestant church, and just how far we had pushed the line of what could seemingly be achieved. So far there had been no repercussions.

3 TOURISTS IN TIRANA

On a warm evening in Thessaloniki, a couple of days after our return from Albania, I sat with Caralee at a pavement café sipping a glass of fresh orange juice and enjoying the faint smell of the sea on the breeze. We had been chatting for a couple of minutes when I noticed a Greek police officer crawling stealthily towards us below the edge of a low stone wall. The man shuffled in closer, reached over the wall and tugged at the edge of my T-shirt. He then pushed back the peak of his cap and shouted, 'Bomb! Bomb!'

I looked across at Caralee, and then around us. We were the only customers left in the café. I glanced along the street, and that too was deserted. I groaned inwardly: a bomb hoax was going to spoil our time together. We drank the remaining juice, reluctantly nodded our consent to the policeman and left him to crawl back the way he had come.

Around ten minutes later, as we sat together at the edge of a nearby park, a huge boom of sound clapped off the walls of the surrounding buildings, sending the birds scattering from the trees. I gripped the edge of the bench for a second. Somehow, though, neither of us felt too shaken up by it. We both seemed to sense God's protection, despite our total obliviousness to any previous bomb warnings. 'And we never paid for our drinks!' I said to Caralee, trying to make light of the situation.

The evening had been an eventful one. Only half an hour before we had reached the café, we had walked right into the middle of a street assault. Two drunken young men were pinning another man to the floor and kicking him viciously in the side. They fled when they saw us. As Caralee went to help the victim and washed his head with some mineral water, the men tentatively began to return, but then changed their minds. It was a frightening situation. We could only guess what they were considering.

Shortly after the bomb blast, I walked Caralee back across the city towards the apartment she was sharing with a couple of friends. We had reached a busy intersection when we heard a tearing screech and a heavy thump next to us on the road. As I turned towards the noise, I saw a man arch high over the bonnet of a car, his motorbike somersaulting slowly after him. They both smacked down heavily on to the tarmac. The cars drew to a standstill, and for a moment the scene seemed to freeze: no one moved from their vehicles. I raced over to the man in the road and checked his tongue to ensure that he could breathe. Shortly afterwards the emergency services arrived. When the man recovered consciousness, however, he began an argument with the police. Other drivers joined in and a huge fracas broke out.

Caralee looked at me, shaking her head. It seemed quite incredible that we should find ourselves in the midst of so many incidents in one evening, and I wondered why it should be so. I took her hand and we wove through the stationary cars to the pavement, and then over to a patch of dry grass at the base of a nearby monument. We sat together, recovering a little composure and looking back at the jammed-up intersection. I glanced at her face: she seemed to be a little ruffled but still at peace. I had been wanting to ask her one question for most of the evening. The words had been running through my head, but somehow I couldn't say them. They came around again, and this time my mouth seized hold of them.

'Caralee. Will you marry me?'

I waited for her to say that she wasn't ready yet, but that wasn't what I heard.

'Yes, I will,' she replied.

For a moment I was shocked; I wondered if I'd heard her right. And then the joy began to flood through all my other feelings. Moments later, we stood up together and walked away from the chaos at the traffic lights, along the white paving flags towards her apartment.

Caralee slept fitfully that night. Later, she told me that as the hours passed in the darkness, she had sensed God's quiet voice speaking about our future together. The Lord had made it clear to her that, just like that evening, our lives would meet unexpected circumstances, traumatic events and dangerous situations. Many of these would be beyond our resources or ability to deal with, but through them all God would give us his peace, protection and help. He had been with us through the evening, and he would be so in future years. Perhaps I did not think about this too closely at the time, for it boded a way ahead that was far from any comforting prospect.

A further sortie to Albania was being organized within the first couple of days of our return from Korçë. Once more the plan was to use the same contact arranging tours for the Greek Communists, and to assemble a team for his next excursion inside, which was to be a five-day run taking in the capital, Tirana. This time we were going to see just how big an outreach we could do with the help of our refugee friends. Almost all the Christian organizations in Thessaloniki were now sending along representatives for the trip: OM, YWAM, People International and Every Home Crusade were to work together, and Caralee and I were to head up the team of around thirty.

On a sunny morning early in June, the coach pulled out through the dry and dusty suburbs of the Greek city. After a couple of hours we were winding up the mountain road to the border crossing, and shortly after we were back on the birch-lined boulevard into Korçë. At the Hotel Iliria this time there was no restraining any of us: team members scattered away into the back-streets in all directions to visit refugee contacts. The driver shrugged his shoulders at the situation and settled in the foyer, playing games of cards. The security officers threw their hands in the air, at a loss as to who exactly they should tail and monitor. Their zeal for the Communist system was now noticeably shaky.

Later that afternoon, Caralee and I met up with Ardian at his apartment. He was the young man who had boldly stepped forward to translate for us in the park. As his mother brought us glasses of raki and a bowl of sweets on a little silver tray, his father came in, wearing a light grey uniform; his face somehow seemed a little familiar. Ardian introduced him as the chief of the town's rapid response police. As I shook his hand nervously, a connection snapped together in my head about what had happened at the rear of the crowd nine days earlier. It had been Ardian's father who had arrived with his men to break up our meeting, only to discover his own son giving his testimony at the centre of it!

'If it hadn't been for my Ardian, I'd have brought in more officers to make sure we broke past the army,' he explained with a grin, waving his hands around emphatically. 'So, if you want to do this kind of thing again, you can do it in our football stadium, and then my men will police it for you!'

I turned to look at Caralee in mute astonishment. We'd had the deepest of concerns about the reaction of the authorities:

only five months earlier, possession of a New Testament in Albania could have got you five years in prison. Now it seemed that allegiances were up in the air and help was being offered to us at the highest level.

We agreed to Ardian's father's proposal, and promised that somehow we'd be back from Tirana to lead the rally in four days' time. If a door had opened, huge as it was, then why not go ahead and step through it?

Back at the hotel, I put it to the rest of the team. Everyone was in agreement. Yet the only resources we had were our small drama team and one sketchboard: we felt ridiculously under-equipped. How on earth we were going to pull it off, only God above knew.

The coach left Korçë the following day on the tour itinerary to Tirana. We bounced along for six long hours, past wide grey rocky riverbeds and huge industrial complexes and along a spectacular ridge north of Elbasan where the pylons marched away over the peaks below us. Once again, our faces were ever fixed on the country rolling by. I kept wondering how we could hope to make a half-reasonable presentation in a football stadium, and whether the venue might not be just a shade out of our league. My head was thumping with a list of unanswerable questions.

In Tirana's only tourist hotel, overlooking the proud statue of Scanderbeg, we met a Dutch youth group who for many months had been preparing the ground for an outreach event in the city's youth park. They invited our team to join them that afternoon. The mood among us was such that they couldn't have stopped us if they'd tried; everyone was game to seize each opportunity presented. Later that afternoon, though, as the rain drizzled down over the empty expanses of grass and we gathered beneath the branches of a large willow tree to pray, the weather seemed to be weighing heavily on our dampened spirits. I felt some words of encouragement were needed.

'We've all seen how God helps us in our work,' I began, glancing around the large circle of people. 'Think of how Ardian just stepped out of the crowd in Korçë … and why should we expect anything less? Hasn't God promised to be with us as we move out in faith? We know that he will guide us and give us the words that we need. So come on! Let's be bold!'

As we set off, the drizzle subsided and the clouds parted, as if the sun shone down its blessing.

The teams gathered on a concrete podium which, until Tirana's students had wrenched it down a couple of months earlier, had supported a towering statue of Stalin. Over the next forty minutes, the musicians and drama team attracted a growing crowd that spread back for around two hundred metres, from the foot of the steps to the trees. Caralee preached a short message with a member of the Dutch team translating. As she did so, I noticed once again that the faces of those listening could clearly be seen to be choosing for or against us, some yielding and some hardening, just as they had in the park in Korçë.

Then it was my turn. The crowd was now standing in a quietness that was a little strange. I could feel the hairs on the back of my neck begin to stand up. I felt suddenly electrified, and I was shaking. I looked back at the podium, smashed free of its once seemingly indomitable icon, and then down at the faces of the Albanians who for almost half a century had been denied any knowledge of God by their rulers' militant atheism. I knew what I had to say.

'For many, many years, your government told you, like Stalin and Marx, that God was dead. Well, I bring you greetings today from a God who is alive and living, a God who has seen the rise and fall of Communism, a system which may soon be dead and buried itself.'

I paused for a moment to look round the crowd. 'Many of you may now be thinking that democracy is the answer.

Democracy is not the answer. Christ, and Christ only, can be the hope for your nation. Many of you may now be thinking of visas, dollars and foreign shores. Well, let me tell you about a man who had all that he wanted, with riches beyond measure, and yet he still found he needed something else ...' and I began to tell the story of the rich young ruler.

Five minutes later, when I had finished, the reaction left me breathless. There was one huge roar, like a gasp of sudden conviction, and cries of 'Po ... Po ... Po ...' It was beyond anything the preaching alone could have achieved. Soon, as we handed out copies of the Gospel of John, the crowd began pushing forward and reaching over the heads of those in front, as if we had brought them the last bread handout from the aid lorry.

I walked around the rear of the crowd to see what was happening on the fringes, and I was overcome by the sight. Hundreds of people were sitting weeping on the grass, stunned by a conviction of truth that they had never conceived of before. My eyes began to smart and I wiped away my own tears on my sleeve. Then I felt a frustration that there were so few among our teams who spoke Albanian and who could counsel these people. We did not have the workers for the harvest. All we could do was to talk with some as best we could and trust the rest to God.

That afternoon, time and motion seemed to slow down to freeze-frame, intensifying the moments as we walked around. God had swept through the hearts of the crowd like a holy wind, such was the level of hunger and readiness among them. We were witnessing the conception of the Albanian church, and I shook my head in awe that our teams were being used to effect it.

Events now quickly took a radical direction. As I walked through the crowd, the people drew back around a man who stepped forward with an air of importance. He turned out to be the country's deputy defence minister, and he was clearly moved at his son's tears and new profession of faith. I talked with them both for a while, and then I felt prompted to make a bold request. 'Can you help us get back to Korçë? We need to return there quickly!'

The man graciously nodded his consent. 'A friend of ours will drive you,' he replied.

I knew that this meeting was a special work of divine happenstance. There were fewer than 150 private cars in the city, and we did not want to risk using a government taxi. The minister's other son, Donald, spoke excellent English. 'Could you meet us in Korçë? We need you!' I appealed. Donald nodded warmly too.

In the dawn light of the following morning, Caralee and I waited uneasily outside the hotel entrance for the driver to collect us. The lobby had been quiet; the waitresses had yet to begin laying the tables for breakfast. I stood watching the fountains in the empty square, glancing at my watch and looking across to the grey stone columns of the opera house.

A battered blue Lada drew up slowly at the kerb. 'Jani?' the driver enquired. I reached in through the window and shook his hand. 'Korçë?' he said.

'Korçë, *shpejtë*,' I replied. I pulled the rear door handle and we quickly slid across the worn seat. He swung the steering wheel sharply to the left and accelerated away.

Caralee and I were both nervous about the move we were making, breaking away from the organized tour schedule, but we had talked it over with other members of our team and felt that it was necessary. Someone needed to be in Korçë early to prepare the ground in advance. The others were going to continue on the scheduled tour circuit, leaving Albania close to the southern town of Gjirokaster, and would meet us back in Korçë in a couple of days with a revitalized team.

Round about midday, the car drew steadily up a long winding ascent and we jolted forward on a tight corner as our driver forced the stick into a lower gear. I looked over the road's edge at the patchwork of fields beneath us and at the high rocky ridges above. Small clusters of stone cottages with their roofs of flaking tiles sat on the flanks of the hills, and nearby a group of workers in their drab clothing were stooped over a patch of land. Now I sensed that God was speaking to me: ideas and words grew loud in my spirit and held me with a deep conviction. I thought about Paul's first letter to the Corinthians, about the Lord 'choosing the foolish to confound the wise', and how few things seemed less foolish than this anarchic country.

'The people are like sheep without a shepherd everywhere you look,' I heard a quiet voice inside me say. 'I am going to do an incredible work in Albania, and you can be a part of it if you choose.'

I couldn't keep back my tears. There was no way I was going to do anything else but be here and be a part of it. I sensed God saying that what was going to happen in Korçë would be big: 'You are going to need to trust me every step of the way, so stay close, Ian.'

I wiped my face quickly and looked at Caralee, but I couldn't share it with her yet. Soon the car rose up over the summit, and a huge expanse of water stretched out below us, with high mountain peaks beyond mirrored perfectly on its surface. It was one of the lakes I had seen from the aeroplane. Soon we were rocking along a pot-holed road on the shore of its beautifully clear waters and through the small town of Pogradec. By the roadside, a blue stencilled sign tilting on its pole read 'Korçë 40km'.

We booked ourselves into the Hotel Iliria again that night and reserved rooms for the returning team. After I had contacted some of the refugees to set the preparations in motion as early as possible, we retired to our beds a little tense and completely exhausted. The following morning, I checked the situation with Ardian's father. The town's football stadium was reserved, and the rapid response police would be deployed to keep order among any crowds that gathered.

Early in the afternoon, when the Communist tour bus rumbled in from Thessaloniki with a reshuffled team on board, preparations began to roll. We gathered together, making our base in a secluded section of the lobby on some old brown leather couches. Even there I sensed that there were eyes observing us, and I wondered if the Sigurimi might still swoop in and break up our meeting.

We knew we needed to publicize the event, and fast: we had only 24 hours to do it. A group was despatched to find some paper and pens to create a batch of posters. They returned an hour later, saying the only place they could find some had been the local printing works – and the manager there had offered to print the posters for us! When they were finished, we began attaching them to walls, windows and trees around the town. It was an excellent start. Word soon reached us that the local radio station had seen them and was interested in the event. A group left to give their testimonies and publicize the stadium gathering through what became a series of broadcasts to the town's population.

One refugee, Alban, reported back to us in the lobby, his eyes wide with excitement, that the town's cinema manager was willing to screen *The Jesus Film*, which we had used in Thessaloniki. It was an unprecedented opportunity, but there wasn't a single copy of the film in the country! It seemed that we had to take a further leap of faith; so we decided to do it. We sent word back that we would screen the film at 6.30 p.m., and sent runners to the radio station to announce it. The cart was firmly before the horse, and we now had to see if we could get a copy – and get it in time. There was also the problem of whether the Albanians would allow it into their country: such things were still 'officially' banned, under severe penalty. But the Communists had prohibited everything we were trying, so why not try this as well? We telephoned Linda in Thessaloniki, and she said she would try to get a copy dispatched to the border immediately. Caralee left the hotel in a taxi late in the afternoon to collect it, and the team gathered together to pray once more that somehow everything would come together. 'O Lord,' I prayed, 'can we possibly pull all this off, and then be allowed to leave?'

Around an hour before the scheduled screening, Caralee returned, breathless, racing across the lobby. I was so relieved to see her. 'Oh Ian,' she gasped, 'the Greek border guards … they searched me and they found it! They looked at me in utter disbelief. One of them said to me: "Woman, you want to get yourself killed by those Albanians? You just go right ahead and take it in there!"' She held up a box of metal canisters. 'The other side didn't check it, though,' she grinned. Within hours of deciding to go for it, we had the film, and my heart was pounding with the exhilaration.

Outside the cinema, the people of Korçë had begun to gather in large groups on the opposite side of the street. I could see already that there were far more wanting to see the film than there were seats inside the building. As Donald, the deputy defence minister's son, and I entered a dingy little office below the projection room, the cinema manager was slouched against the wall. He motioned for us to sit. I could smell the vodka on his breath and see the cynical look in his eyes. He said a few words in Albanian and then shrugged his shoulders.

'He says that he is sorry, but that it's not possible for him to show the film. He has changed his mind,' said Donald, the irritation showing in his voice. 'It is too big a thing. He says that some people have threatened him if he does it. He is afraid.'

'Tell him that he said that he would,' I replied firmly, 'and that we have announced it on the radio across the town and gone to considerable trouble to get it here.'

The man held up his hands in appeal and spoke again. 'He is saying that he can't. It's too much!' said Donald. I looked down and shook my head.

We left the office and stood for a moment in the entrance foyer. Donald looked at me and raised his eyebrows. Outside, the crowd had grown even larger, and they were now tapping on the patchy glass doors to come in. I could feel my palms getting sticky. Some of the other workers in our party had arrived, and we held a quick discussion.

As we prayed, I sensed God guiding us clearly about what we should do: 'Go and tell him that you are going to show it whether he likes it or not!' It was a pretty authoritative line to take. I gulped a little at the prospect of saying it, and I glanced around the group. Then Donald turned the door handle and we walked back into the office.

The man had been sitting at his desk fidgeting. I looked at him squarely and addressed him: 'Tell him that we believe God wants to show this film tonight …' I paused for a moment. 'It is not a question of what he wants to do, but whether he is going to do what God wants.' I felt a growing confidence as I spoke. Donald translated.

The man ran his hand around his collar and the colour drained from his face. He muttered a few words in reply. Donald looked back at me.

'He says: "How is God going to make him?"'

'There are at least eight hundred people waiting outside to see this film,' I replied. 'Does he want us to go into the street and let them all know that he is afraid to show it?'

The man sat back in his chair. 'Oh,' he said. That I understood. Moments later, he flicked his finger with grudging resignation. We had the go-ahead.

When the cinema doors opened the people filed in, eyeing us foreigners with a mixture of suspicion and awe as they passed. I glanced around the venue at the dirty cream walls, the tatty velvet seats and the screen curtain hanging perilously on its rail, but it didn't dampen my expectations. The rows filled up quickly, with people sitting on each other's knees and on the aisle floors, shouting and waving at each other. Soon the lights were dimmed, the beam from the projector shone down through the darkness, and the noise began to die down. There were no seats left, so I made my way back to the entrance area.

Outside, many more people were waiting, hoping that they too could gain entrance for the screening. I sat with a group of team members and prayed for the film to make a big impact upon all those inside, but my thoughts kept turning to the next day at the football stadium and what exactly we could do in such a large venue – we didn't even have a programme, or a sound-system, for that matter.

In a little while, I heard the sound of many people gasping from inside the cinema hall. I turned to look around. One of the team jogged over to the entrance and peered inside. 'It was the resurrection scene,' he called back. The film was almost over.

Soon people began to file out of the darkness of the hall. Many were wiping the tears from their faces. In the foyer and outside on the pavement they hovered around aimlessly, glancing at each other and us. For many it was as if the ground had shifted beneath them, and they did not know where to tread next. The team was prepared and we mingled among them. We gave out copies of the Gospels and tracts, and told as many people as we could to come to the football stadium the next day, fumbling with our best attempts at Albanian: 'Stadium … nesër … ora… katër …'

I felt a growing anxiety throughout the following morning as we worked together to assemble a programme for the football stadium, packed on the tatty leather couches in our corner of the lobby. Most things seemed to be coming together as we brainstormed ideas, with the exception of one pretty crucial feature. We had hastily managed to translate a couple of songs from English into Albanian, and had written out the words in 18-inch-high black lettering on pieces of paper from the printing works so we could lead the crowd in worship. We had our drama team ready and waiting. We had our sketchboard ready to paint some visuals, as inadequate as it would be, and we had refugees who were more than willing to step out in public and share their own personal stories of how they had been changed by God's love. The problem was, how would anyone hear a word we said?

It was a difficulty that we should have anticipated God would solve for us. At around midday, a rather weasel-faced man sought us out at the hotel. He had seen the posters for the event, and said he was calling to enquire if we might need a sound system: he could, if we wanted, arrange for one to be transported over from the town's Palace of Culture! There was no hesitation in our reply, and all around the couches there were wide grins. For the whole weekend, it seemed that obstacles were being cleared from the path ahead of us. Like many others on the team, I thanked God deeply in my heart.

Ardian's father had brought in around two hundred officers, stationed along the approach road and dotted around the stadium's terraces. The men stood alert in their high black boots, clutching regulation Kalashnikov rifles. Ardian's father hovered near the entrance gates, smiling with pride at the operation he had mounted. It was impressive, but I wondered if it might not prove a little intimidating for the town's people.

With just half an hour to go before the scheduled start time, there were very few people inside the stadium and I felt that my concerns might, frustratingly, be right. Nevertheless, we set up the sketchboard and carefully laid out the song words in order along the white sideline, and shortly the weaselly man from the Palace of Culture arrived with a sound system rocking around in the back of a van.

My relief at his arrival was tempered when I saw the actual equipment. Wires were tumbling out of the back of a battered black box, all twisted and taped together in a disturbing weave of colour. We set it up and tested it out, and it was still, miraculously, in working order. By now the terraces were filling up rapidly, and I felt my stomach tighten.

By the time to start, the ground had filled up to its capacity, with people standing up to twenty deep all around the stepped concrete terracing. I figured there must be around five thousand people chattering and shuffling shoulder to shoulder under the watchful gaze of Ardian's father's men. I felt both amazed and humbled that we were actually in this situation – so far beyond anything that anyone had conceived might be possible a month earlier. Now we would see what would happen. I stepped up to the microphone and addressed the crowd.

'*Mirë dita*, ladies and gentlemen. We are a team of Christians from many different countries, including Albania, and we have an important message for you to hear today ...' The sound system cracked and let out a high-pitched whine. The hum of voices died down, and the programme got under way.

The crowd listened attentively to the refugees telling their stories of how their lives had been turned around in Thessaloniki by their new knowledge of God. They watched the drama team perform on the grass and the presentation that Caralee made, swiftly dabbing paint on the sketchboard. How much they could actually see, I was unsure about. What seemed to matter most, though, was that we had their attention and that they could hear us. Later, team members grouped close to the sideline to hold up song lyrics on the paper sections. The crowd joined in as our singers led on the microphone, at first a little cautiously, but then with a growing willingness that seemed to build into conviction.

Because he lives, I can face tomorrow,
Because he lives, all fear is gone.
Because I know, I know he holds the future,
And life is worth living, just because he lives.

As I watched, I could see that many were now no longer just watching. People were punching the air as they sang the words 'all fear is gone'. It was as if in that moment their fear had been broken: their fear of us foreigners, their fear of the authorities, their fear of the future. The time had come for us to make an appeal.

I now felt highly expectant but still uncertain of how people would respond. I stepped up to the microphone and invited those who felt ready to follow God to come forward and take a copy of the Gospel of John. For thirty long seconds, the people were motionless. Then suddenly they started to leap over the perimeter barrier in ones and twos and ran towards us at a furious pace, and after that the terraces seemed to pour down on to the grass like water released through irrigation gates. When the first runners arrived, they clasped their copies like a treasured possession. As more skidded in behind them, they began reaching over each other with their arms outstretched, forming wild, boisterous huddles. The huddles closed in on the team members, who were digging frantically into their sacks of books, and swamped them. One of our workers, a small Swedish guy with near-white hair, surfaced from the crowd like an air-filled bottle from water, and was passed bobbing over their heads. When the books were all taken the crowds dispersed a little, and an announcement was made that the meeting was over.

Out of the corner of my eye, I noticed that the sound system was now smoking heavily. It seemed that its wires had been capable of sustaining one last surge of life, and this had burnt it out.

As we tried to walk back through the centre of Korçë towards the hotel, we were mobbed. Crowds of people surrounded us and jogged alongside, smiling and laughing, patting us on the back and jostling with each other to hold on to our hands or shirt sleeves. We might have been the town's football team bringing home some major national trophy, but our victory, I felt, had been the breaking down of so much fear in Korçë hearts. People were now emptying out of cafés on to the pavement and opening their windows above our heads as we passed. I noticed many others, however, whose coolness could be felt as they stood at a distance, angered by what was taking place. I knew that many of those who were surrounding us would perhaps slip away from the hope that they had seized, but I felt that the kindling of something more in the town was only just beginning. It was a truly astonishing moment, and I was floating high on the exhilaration of it all.

That evening, the team fanned out into the town's homes, meeting and greeting our contacts and converts. I waited up until 2.30 a.m., watching the hotel entrance doors from our couch in the lobby to make sure everyone returned safely. By 7.30 that morning we had left Korçë behind us, the dust off the back of the coach trailing away over the green fields and the gun bunkers.

4 DOWN HOME AMONG
THE GUN BUNKERS

On a bitterly cold day in January 1992, I sat in the passenger seat of our Land-Rover as Caralee drove us cautiously back along the icy road from the Kapshtice border crossing to the town of Korçë. The fields on either side of us were covered in a thick layer of snow, and the silver birch trees that had swayed in the breeze of the previous spring had disappeared, for mile after mile. Only their stumps remained, pushing up from beneath the powdery white blanket. We were to learn that during the previous months they had all been chopped down for firewood by the people. No one had prevented what was a terrible diminishment of the countryside. Anarchy was now widespread throughout Albania.

We were returning to Korçë to live, and I felt a buzz of excitement that we were finally arriving. The town had seemed like the natural destination for us: it was here that God had blessed our work and made the heart of the most fruitful and remarkable events. We had picked up a second-hand Land-Rover with mushy-pea-green paintwork in Bristol, loaded it with clothes, bed linen, tinned food and diesel canisters, and driven overland via Italy to avoid the escalating conflict in Yugoslavia. Bob Atkin had driven along behind us with a lorry full of medicines and beds for the town's hospital. Since the week of the gathering at Korçë football stadium, we had returned on a number of other visits to Albania to strengthen our contacts, but our plan had been to make a permanent move here when the time was right.

Caralee had sensed God's call to Albania in her own special moment. She had always felt that she would work in Africa, but when someone had remarked that in many ways Albania was like a little bit of Africa in the heart of Europe, a further piece of her life fell into place. I had told her about my own experience of God speaking to me as we had ridden in the battered Lada through the mountains southeast of Tirana. Our lives were united in calling.

We had shared our vision with a number of churches in England and with the organization that had trained us, Open Air Campaigners. The reactions, however, had not always been affirming. Many had raised their concerns. Is it right to send a young couple into the heart of a dangerous and unstable country? How prepared are they? Maybe they should wait? My father had let me know that he thought it was a crazy thing to do with my life. 'You might just end up getting yourselves killed!' my mother had exclaimed.

Though I felt the pressure of these remarks, I was under no doubt about where I should be and when. I had never felt so sure of anything in my life. To me the Lord's call had an urgency about it. Why spend months raising financial support for our plans? We had been pledged a small amount of money from some sources, and believed that he would provide along the way that he was leading.

Caralee and I had been married the previous December in San Jose, California. I was 28 years old and Caralee, a dietician with an Armenian father, was two years my senior. We had spent a rushed two-week honeymoon visiting Yosemite National Park, San Francisco and Disneyland in the crisp winter weather.

While meeting up with Caralee's old friends and relatives, a very special thing happened for me. A sensitive woman by the name of Betsy Reeves had organized an impromptu reunion in Fresno, Caralee's former university town, for a group of her old travelling friends. It was at Betsy's house, among this remarkable collection of individuals who seemed so open and dedicated to Christ's service, that I felt embraced in fellowship by people truly like-minded in their outlook. We listened to their testimonies of triumph and struggle and they listened to us explain our calling, and there I felt that we were fully understood. I felt I had been adopted into a new Christian family. Many of the people we met in Fresno pledged us their support, at that time not in dollars but with encouragement and prayer backing. They also offered to send out teams to work with us over the coming summer, and it gave us both a tremendous lift.

We arrived in Korçë with no accommodation arranged. Within a week, though, we had rented the upstairs of a house belonging to a refugee's relative. The neighbourhood was a pleasant, cobbled part of the town known as Little Paris. Our home was to be a medium-sized single room with an attached kitchenette, and it was painted with the same salmon pink and lime green colour scheme that everyone else in the town had – they were the only colours available! We were to share our 'squatover' toilet with the family downstairs. It was, true to say, a very modest dwelling, but no worse than the majority of Korçë residents were used to.

The first two things we purchased for our new life together were a small Bulgarian stove to heat our tinned and packet food and an ineffectual electric radiator to try to heat the room. The temperature, outside and in, was well below freezing in daytime, and colder still at night. It seemed sometimes that I could see my breath even in the darkness. During our first months there, we spent the nights huddled together wearing three sets of clothing under half a dozen blankets to keep warm enough for sleep. One morning, I remember noticing a street fountain frozen mid-flow, like some children's cartoon, and touching it to be sure it was real.

Mike Brown, the fair-haired missionary who had accompanied us on the Greek Communist bus, had moved into Korçë several months earlier. Mike had helped gather up respondents and returning refugees into a large Bible study group that began meeting every Monday night in the town's dusty Palace of Culture. Daylight meetings with foreigners were still a risk. Here we found a number of old friends, and together we met regularly to worship and study the Bible with the help of those who spoke a little English, while we tried our best to learn more basic Albanian phrases. Ligor, known by everyone as Xhaxhi (uncle) Ligor, the old man who had knocked on our hotel door late at night, was present, but Koci Treska had now passed away, content, we were told, with the events he had awaited for so many years.

We now witnessed at first hand how hard life was for the people of Albania. The few shops that existed, trading out of premises with little or no window glass (the factories had all ceased producing it) had little to sell except leeks and jars of fig jam. Ration cards were needed even for these. For many, their daily meal was a slice of bread and butter sprinkled with sugar. The collapsing Communist system was miserably failing to feed the country. We were forced to make regular forays into Greece to buy the food we needed to get by.

It was a liberty others were denied. I remember accompanying our neighbour at 5.30 a.m. to a bleak, out-of-the-way crossroads for a bread delivery. The queue already waiting there was huge. When the bread lorry rumbled in, I stumbled back in amazement as the crowd fought in desperation for the loaves of bread. There simply wasn't enough to go around. In their anger they hoisted the truck by the wheel arches and toppled it crashing on to its side. The driver clambered out, holding the side of his head and cursing the crowd furiously.

During our first month in Korçë, as we tried to sleep, we could hear intermittent bursts of gunfire: a 'tat-tat-tat' punctuating the passage of the early hours. Caralee and I hugged each other to sleep; we had never experienced such things before. When daylight came, the victims of the violence would be found cold and slumped in the streets. Everyone in the neighbourhood would talk about the latest incident, and explanations would usually emerge. The killings were political in motive, and were spinning backwards and forwards across factions in cycles of revenge. Sometimes it was individuals being shot by the secret police, the Sigurimi, for trying to start opposition political movements, or people taking revenge on Sigurimi and the Communists.

Elections were soon to be held, and groups were jockeying for power with intimidation and terror. One night we were woken by an explosion booming along a nearby street. Caralee and I clasped each other in the darkness and sat up, listening to the shouts and screams. 'O Lord,' I prayed, 'keep us secure under your wing.' The next day, I came across a patch of cobblestones wet with blood. The walls on either side of it were peppered with shrapnel marks. We later learnt that a particularly hated member of the Sigurimi had been dragged out of his home and grenaded. Initially, it was all deeply disturbing, but as the weeks passed we grew uncomfortably accustomed to it.

After a short while settling into life in Korçë, we felt ready for the next phase of our work. We had not come into Albania to settle within a group of new believers, but to try to reach out constantly with the message of God's saving love. Hidden from view in the mountains and valleys in all directions out of Korçë were hundreds of rural villages. We pinned up a map on the pink wall in our room and determined that we would visit as many of them as we could. A team of new Albanian believers willing to come along with us quickly grew, and we began the task in earnest, colour-coding our campaign area with red and blue pens: red for virgin territory and blue for places we deemed ready for further follow-up. Almost every day began with prayer meetings in our room, and then we would fill up the back of the Land-Rover with people squashing in on top of each other and sitting on wooden planks jammed against the walls.

Among others, Holger and Xhaxhi Berti became regular co-workers on these campaigns. Holger was an intelligent young English teacher with a well-trimmed beard and a considered manner of speaking. He had picked up a copy of the Gospel from a visiting YWAM team, and subsequently he and his entire close family had become believers. I remember Holger explaining: 'My parents' advice to me was "always find a friend better than yourself".' As an exceptional student, he had always struggled to find such a friend, but in Jesus he had at last met the person worthy of his parents' adage. Holger became my right-hand translator.

'Uncle' or Xhaxhi Berti, a hollow-cheeked man with a flap of hair reaching over his bald head like a tentacle, arrived at our Bible studies with endless questions. He would always remain behind to ask more and more questions, sometimes repeating them intensely. I had initially thought he might be a little crazy, until I learnt more about him. Berti had spent 29 years of his life imprisoned, six of them in solitary confinement, and had only recently been released. His initial sentence for protesting against the government had been for two years, but this just kept getting extended. Before he went into solitary, he had learnt the Lord's Prayer from a Catholic priest. 'I read it and I kept it in my mind, repeating it again and again and again,' he told me, with the lines of concentration darkening on his forehead. Saying it over and over had kept him sane. Alone in his cell, he had met the Lord and saved up his years of questions. Now that he had found our growing church, he devoured biblical knowledge like a famished soul.

Berti grew and grew in his faith, and so did his passion to tell others about God. When he wasn't with us in the Land-Rover, he rode around the villages on his bicycle on his own unstoppable one-man campaign.

As we bounced along the mud and stone tracks towards our destinations, often for up to three hours at a time, we worshipped as we drove. A sweet spirit of praise helped keep up our spirits. Holger's brother-in-law, Ilo, a consummate musician, would play his flute, or Caralee would 'pap-pap-pap' on the horn as she drove, to the Albanian translation of 'I Will Enter His Gates with Thanksgiving in My Heart'. Sometimes Iliri, a huge ex-drunk, would sing in a bass voice so deep it seemed to make the metal sides of the Land-Rover reverberate.

In most villages we would set up at a central point, and Ilo would draw the residents out of their homes like the Pied Piper. Usually, however, the sight of the Land-Rover was enough to attract a crowd; most people had never seen such a vehicle before in their lives, let alone any foreigners. We made sketchboard presentations, preached short messages and shared our testimonies. With the children we played games, told stories, sang songs, chanted memory verses and taught them how to pray. We handed out boot-loads of tracts and Gospels, and later, as we returned to places for a second time, we would show the film *The Life of Jesus* on a portable TV-video recorder. Where faith took root, we encouraged the villagers to begin meeting together. Those who translated and travelled with us soon became trained and led the meetings themselves.

As the months went past, I felt on a continuous high. Though the work was draining, we saw people responding daily with interest and tears, and that made the long Land-Rover journeys worth it. On one occasion we visited a remote village high in the mountains where the houses were built of brown mud, terraced steeply down the hillside to a fast-flowing milky-white beck. As I looked down on to the houses, I could see through the patchy roofing to the interiors where the villagers shared certain rooms with their livestock. A smell of damp soil and animal dung was thick in the air. Unusually, no one came out to meet us as we walked down the cobbled lane; all was quiet except for the odd cluck of a hen. I was conscious, however, of many eyes upon us, peeping out timidly from behind curtains and through the latticed branch fencing. The people seemed like a separate shy tribe.

Caralee gave out copies of the New Testament door-to-door, and spent time in the home of a woman named Bukuria. The woman's skin was dark and leathery, and like everyone in the villages she wore many layers of worn clothing to keep out the cold.

'I'd like to share with you from this book, which is God's word,' Caralee explained. 'He has some special things that he wants you to know about him. Can we read with you?'

Villagers would often offer the customary hospitality and then remain constantly on the move bringing out tiny glasses of plum raki and bowls of *llokume* (Turkish Delight), but Burukia began to listen attentively. As Caralee read the Scriptures to her, she kept asking for more and more, and then enquired about Caralee and the other Albanians with us and why they believed in this God. It was as if a spiritual thirst was awakening in her that she hadn't known she possessed. The woman's bright blue eyes lit up as sections of the Bible were explained to her.

As Caralee left, Bukuria took off a string of toy pearls and placed them around her neck. Her eyesight was poor, so we tried to arrange for someone else in the village to read to her. We knew that something very important had happened for Bukuria that day, and Caralee too was deeply touched by the meeting.

We had been visiting a village called Dishnicë, a ten-minute drive out of Korçë, running regular programmes for the children, when a couple approached us holding their tiny, blonde-haired daughter in their arms.

'We hear that you are people of God,' the mother appealed. 'Will you come and pray for our *çupa* Majlinda?' The child had a condition that had prevented her from ever walking, and the family had consulted the medical profession widely in the area and found no remedy. Caralee and I, Xhaxhi Berti and two young Albanian boys from the fellowship in Korçë prayed with them, and then later Xhaxhi and the boys returned to petition God again. The following week, the little girl was smiling and pushing a little wooden walking frame on wheels as she tottered around. The parents were ecstatic with joy – and so were we. After Xhaxhi and the boys continued to pray, the girl made a complete recovery, and later she ran into our meetings with abandon. It was not that I didn't believe God capable of such things, but I'd never witnessed them before.

Because Xhaxhi and the boys had taken up the prayer baton, the event was significant in another way. It broke down the idea in the growing church in Korçë that prayer needed to come from us 'holy' foreigners to be really effective. As others now began to pray with new confidence, we saw many more people healed of their complaints and afflictions.

Our visits to the villages always generated interest, but sometimes it wasn't quite so positive. As we drew into the village of

Pirg, on the road north to Lake Pogradec, old Ligor, who had expressed a particular interest in joining us for the day, suddenly opened the door of the vehicle and jumped out on to the dirt road.

'Where's he going?' I exclaimed, glancing around. No one else could answer. We hadn't even parked the vehicle, let alone set up our equipment for the programme, but Ligor held up his Bible as the curly-haired villagers quickly gathered around him and began to preach at them with passion.

Next minute, as I walked across with some of the others to join him, a rock landed on the earth close to his feet, sending up a little dust cloud. Ligor looked across at me and began to edge away steadily. I could see other people now stooping down and picking up rocks. As he ran back towards us, the stones began to fly and shower the ground around us.

'Get back to the Land-Rover, quickly!' I shouted. As we all turned and ran, the rocks came bouncing along the road after us. One of them struck my shoulder, sending a sharp pain into my back as I stumbled towards the car. As we accelerated away, one final rock thumped down on to the roof, bidding us good riddance with a full stop on the end. Ligor turned to me as we sped back along the main road to Korçë.

'Yes,' he said shaking his head. 'That village was the same fifty years ago when we came here as a youth group.'

'Why didn't you tell us, Ligor?' I exclaimed, rubbing my surfacing bruise.

'I had to try again,' he replied. I had to respect his willingness after half a century. The village had remained trenchantly Communist, despite the shifting currents in the country's ideology and the Democratic Party's victory in the March elections. In Pirg and other places, our faith was still viewed as an unwelcome Western decadence, an opium and a crutch.

We continued our work in the villages that June, bolstered by a team of helpers from Caralee's old church, First Presbyterian in Fresno. Their presence was a huge lift to Caralee and me, and many of the new Albanian believers also felt a link to the worldwide church in a way they had never done before. Together we visited around thirty villages with evangelistic programmes, gathering up those who responded into small groups. Along the way, we kept one eye open for a location ripe for a church plant, and we settled on Progër, a village at the foot of a high ridge of mountains, just off the border road. Holger, the English teacher, worked at the village school; its director was in our fellowship and a number of its teenagers had also become believers.

We set about renovating Progër village school in August, with the help of a team of workers from Bristol and California. As well as being a form of service to the community, we knew it would give us a platform from which to speak more directly into the villagers' lives. Like so many buildings in the country, the school was in a terribly decrepit condition. It had little window glass remaining, the woodwork was crumbling, the paintwork was peeling, the furniture was broken and the electrics needed completely rewiring. It was a wonder that the pupils learnt anything in such conditions, but somehow they did.

Our teams joined together with local craftsmen, villagers, teachers and even some of the pupils themselves to renovate it completely. We repaired the woodburning stoves, re-rendered the outside walls, replaced the floorboards, fitted new doors and locks, had furniture built locally, repainted the entire building inside and out, and undertook a heap of other jobs!

The school had been adorned inside with a range of Communist slogans. In the Russian classroom, 'A foreign language is a weapon in the struggle of life' was emblazoned across the wall. I took a particular pleasure in slapping a thick coat of paint over such phrases. With the director's consent, we replaced them with biblical proverbs, like 'He who walks in wisdom will be secure', and commissioned an artist to cover a mural of Enver Hoxha with a large descending dove of peace. It seemed deeply poignant.

When all the work was finished, the school was, condition-wise, one of the best in the state.

As we worked on the building's fabric, we held children's and teenagers' programmes, with up to a hundred in attendance at a time, and gave out New Testaments to every home. Progër was filled with worship music every day, and a new, lighter spirit affected everyone there. At the end of the project, we knew of around a dozen new people who had made commit-ments to follow Christ, including the head of the village, and a group was duly begun.

To inaugurate the school, we held a public meeting one evening in the rich and reddening sunlight, and the villagers filled the square for the occasion. I preached a short message, Ligor gave his testimony, and then I noticed Xhaxhi Berti, with his peaked cap tipped upwards, raise his hand and look across at me. Like Ligor, Berti was now a well-known character local-ly, and his 29-year stretch in the Communist prison gave him the highest respect when he spoke. Berti stepped forward, coughed, and then took off his cap. Everyone waited attentively.

'Mirë mbrëma, people of Progër. I'd like to pray for you all,' he announced solemnly. 'O Lord, with you we have the strength – the strength to gallop towards heaven.'

Caralee looked up at me and raised an eyebrow. Berti was irrepressible.

'Lord,' he continued, his voice building with emotion, 'our lives are nothing before you. Earth is nothing and heaven is everything. O Lord, we can't wait to get to heaven. Take us there tonight! I pray that you would take my life tonight … and all my brothers and sisters in Progër … take their lives tonight. Amen!'

Berti repositioned his cap with aplomb. There was a moment of awkward silence. The villagers looked at each other quizzically, and I looked down at my feet to conceal my amusement. For a long time afterwards, the people of Progër would recount how Berti had come along and prayed for them all to die!

The Land-Rover we had driven from England had become vital to our life in Korçë, both to bring food supplies over the border from Greece and to transport our team of Albanian co-workers on our journeys into the surrounding villages. Because there were so few other vehicles in the country, we were regularly targeted by the light-fingered, and sometimes by other forms of unwanted attention on the road. There were times during our days when we felt as if God's hands were clasping ours firmly, and others when we felt that he had let them slip, or that the Enemy had wielded the back of his hand across our faces. The wing mirrors, the chrome trim and the petrol caps would constantly vanish, and because of this we were regularly compelled to leave a guard with the car when we parked up.

On one occasion in Maliq, a new town built on reclaimed land and a little wild in character, we returned to find our guard nowhere in sight – bought off, we suspected. The headlights and indicators had all been unscrewed and the diesel filter had been stolen, as well as all the usual targets being stripped off. I thumped the bonnet as I walked around surveying all the damage. There was little we could do about it, except continue to drive it around in its existing state until we could buy another round of replacements on our next trip to Greece.

We learnt that many of the items being stolen were strangely prized as objects in themselves. Sometimes we would see a rear-view mirror or an orange indicator cover, swiped from some other unfortunate motorist, displayed like an important ornament in a family's living-room cabinet. Most people had so few possessions, and such things were 'Western' and rare. Regularly, following some knocking, rattling or thump, the vehicle would break down miles away from anywhere, on the edge of some pinewoods or overlooking some empty vale silent but for the breeze or the bells of a herd of goats. In the stillness of such moments, our dependence on God's care seemed even more pronounced. I had little idea about the workings of an engine, and we would pray for a solution. Thankfully, the Lord would never leave us there.

Early one evening, as Caralee was driving us home from a village in the mountains, a rusty van drove up dangerously close to our rear. The van then drew back and accelerated level with us on our left, holding its course alongside on the narrow road. I glanced across and saw a group of men peering back at us from the front seat. A bad feeling came over me. The van accelerated past us, pulled back on to the right in front, and then slammed on the brakes to force us to slow down.

'Try to keep moving. Don't stop! That's what they want,' I shouted anxiously, throwing my hands forward on to the dash-board.

'Don't shout at me!' replied Caralee. She swerved around them on to the dirt and kept the vehicle moving slowly.

For the next 20 minutes, the van pulled back in behind us, accelerated close to the bumper, and then overtook and braked. It was impossible to know whether they were playing some thoughtless game or had other criminal intentions. I prayed with a repetitious fervour, and eventually they simply tired of their tactic and turned off the road along a dirt track. We were both shaken up, but over the next few kilometres as we drove along we felt a palpable warmth envelop us like some strong and tender embrace. It was a deeply reassuring moment. If we had not felt God's love so tangibly at this and other times, I think we would have left the country.

Such incidents seemed to posses a greater menace in the climate of lawlessness, but it was not to be the most unsettling. One day, as we were driving home, a man in a car in front of us slid the top half of his body out of the passenger window and sat on the door staring back at us, his brown curly hair streaming over his face in the wind. I watched as he reached back inside the car and drew out a pistol. He then casually clasped his wrist to steady his hold, sited his eye along the barrel and pointed it straight at Caralee.

The moment seemed completely unreal. I couldn't believe what I was seeing. I could hear the blood pumping around my head – I was horrified. The man lowered the pistol and grinned. He then jerked it upward with mock recoil, as if he had just fired it. Caralee slowed the Land-Rover down and the car drew away down the road. She sat silently with the colour draining from her face. I held her for a couple of minutes. I was shaking and furious.

Back in Korçë, I reported the incident to the police, and as it transpired the Lord worked through the incident in more ways than one. The man in charge of the investigation, an athletic-looking character in a neatly pressed suit who introduced himself as Captain Zylyftari, took the matter seriously – never something to be presumed. Over the coming weeks, I became friendly with him, and he eventually caught the culprit, a young soldier. In the manner of Albanian culture, the soldier's relatives made an indirect approach to us for forgiveness. One evening, in the fusty-smelling town police cells, we talked with him for a while. He was remorseful about what he had done, and we were able to tell him about the availability of God's love and forgiveness for everyone. When he was released, he even attended the church fellowship on a couple of occasions, but we sensed that somehow he still felt uncomfortable around us, and there was, regrettably, little more we could do about that.

On a further occasion, we were driving to the small town of Bilisht along the route from Korçë to Kapshtice. The road was covered in a thick layer of compacted snow. We were cornering a bend in the early morning light when the wheels suddenly lost their grip and the Land-Rover veered sharply to the right. The force propelled me clean out of the left-hand passenger door as it swung open. I landed lightly on my side in the snow at the edge of the road, but as I looked back up I saw the Land-Rover falling towards me. It bounced on its side and then back on to its wheels before gyrating to a slow standstill some ten metres away on the opposite side of the road. The whole incident happened in seconds.

As I lay there in the strange silence that followed, I felt shaken and wet but physically fine. Moments later, Caralee and our other passenger, Stavri, ran over towards me. Caralee was shaking and in tears.

'Ian, I don't know what happened. I'm sorry. We just spun! Are you okay?' she said, brushing the snow off my forehead and helping me to sit up.

'Yeah … I think so,' I replied.

Stavri stood motionless, pointing beside me, wide-eyed. The imprint of my frame was defined in the snow like the chalk outline of a body removed from the scene of a crime. Next to it was the huge imprint of the side of the Land-Rover. The distance between them was three inches! I could feel my legs shaking now, but over that grew a sensation of awe. I felt that my life had surely been graciously preserved in the accident. As we walked back along the road to the vehicle, we thanked God again for his protection.

We were to further experience God's special preservation and amazing vindication one spring morning as we attempted to cross over from Albania to Greece along that same road. Caralee and I felt deeply in need of a rest in Thessaloniki. I had been leading a huge number of Bible studies, and the constant stream of visitors from the growing Korçë fellowship to our room in Little Paris, sometimes from 8 a.m. through to 11 p.m., was draining. So was the feeling of living in a fishbowl, being constantly watched by others: along with Mike Brown, we were the only foreigners living in the market town for the region's 250,000 people. Sometimes, when we reached Greece, we would sleep for 24 hours at a stretch to recover.

On this day, when we reached the Greek side of the border, we discovered their customs officers were on strike. I asked a policeman if it was still okay to pass through, and he told me it was fine by him. However, as Caralee began to drive past the customs point, a man in a light grey uniform jumped up on to the footplate, yanked open my door and dragged me down on to the road. As my side hit the ground, he was going berserk, shouting, punching me in the stomach and kicking me in the back and kidneys. I was completely stunned by the assault. Other customs officers were gathering around, and I could hear Caralee screaming at them to stop.

When the beating had finished, my sides were raw and I felt sick and in shock. We were made to park up our vehicle and led away towards a police Land-Rover. We had driven through the customs officers' picket line, and the man, a stocky colonel with a high forehead, was shouting that he was going to have us arrested.

'You have tried to enter our country with violence,' he raged, scarlet-faced. I couldn't believe the accusation. We were driven away from the border point with the colonel and a police officer sitting stiffly in the front. I looked at Caralee: she had tears in her eyes. Two of my ribs were too sensitive to touch, and I didn't know what was going to happen to us. The officer was offering no explanations, and the colonel kept repeating his charge.

After a short drive, the car drew into the Greek town of Kastoria and pulled up outside the courthouse. The colonel marched us roughly inside the building. We sat there waiting for an unbearably long time in a plain room with a single wooden bench. I felt deeply upset and afraid: we were in a foreign country, unable to speak the language and facing a trumped-up charge. Caralee's hand felt warm as I held it, and we prayed together furiously.

The colonel entered shortly and presented us with a document and a black Biro. 'Sign this … here,' he shouted gruffly. It was written in Greek, which neither of us could read, but I assumed it was some admission of our offence. Another policeman was attempting to translate but saying little more than, 'Sign here please.'

As I pushed the document away, my hand was shaking.

'Look,' I said angrily, 'we'd like to speak to a lawyer.'

'You haven't got a lawyer,' the colonel snapped sarcastically. 'You're in Greece now. You'll sign it, or else you'll be forgotten about!' It was an ominous statement.

At that very moment, a tall, olive-skinned man in a blue pin-striped suit entered the room. Under his arm he held a buffed briefcase and an Oxford legal dictionary. 'I'll be your lawyer,' he announced in an upper-class English accent.

No one said a word: everyone was equally stunned. The man spoke quickly in Greek, and the colonel and the officer left the room. He sat down next to Caralee without introducing himself. 'Tell me what has happened,' he said, and I explained the events of the last couple of hours with a huge sense of relief.

'Wait here,' he replied, 'I shan't be long.'

Half an hour later, we entered the courtroom with the man now representing us. 'Sit here with me,' he said. 'You will be all right. Just say that you are sorry when I tell you.'

There were three judges presiding over the session that day in Kastoria courthouse: two men, and a woman sitting in the middle, all of them dressed in black and red legal robes. The policeman spoke first, then the customs colonel, and then our lawyer. The colonel spoke again with a red face, raising his voice angrily. Our lawyer spoke once more, and then the room went silent. Neither Caralee nor I could understand a word of what was being said.

As I waited, I felt tense and cold. I shuffled uncomfortably in the chair and cast my eyes around the room. Directly behind the woman judge was a large Orthodox painting of the resurrected Christ with his arms outstretched towards us. Across the courtroom roof, the painting fanned out to depict a grey-bearded God the Father looking down from a patch of blue sky between the clouds. I studied the painting for a long minute. A strong sensation came over me that in this room Jesus was going to be both our judge and our advocate, and my spirits began to lift.

The woman judge stood up and slammed her hammer down on the bench. She turned towards us and announced: 'You are without blame, and free to go. I'm sorry.' The sense of relief and vindication was phenomenal. She then turned to the colonel and began to berate him at length. He seemed to shrink a little before her and turned even redder in the face.

Outside the courtroom, we shook our lawyer's hand firmly. 'Could we have your card? We still don't know your name,' I enquired. 'What do we owe you?'

'Oh, it's all right,' the man replied, already stepping away. 'You would have done the same for me.' Then he was gone through the front door of the courthouse.

I looked at Caralee and she at me. It was a little strange. The police officer escorted us back to the car, and the colonel sat without speaking in the front. As we drove towards the border, he reached back and offered his hand. I shook it, lightly at first, but then with firmness as he looked at me with his pride now diminished.

The whole incident left a deep impression on us. It seemed to underline in our hearts God's amazing care, even if we strayed over the edge – in this instance through a picket line. And as for our free lawyer who had so quickly disappeared, who was he? An angel with an Oxford legal dictionary?

The next time we arrived at the border, the colonel greeted me like an old friend, hugging me warmly and offering me a glass of ouzo. It was as if, like children, we'd had a fight and made up and now he respected me. Whenever I needed help getting people or goods through the border from then on, it was the colonel's pleasure to make the process smooth.

During our first year in Korçë, we heard rumours of an orphanage and took a group of people from the fellowship to visit it. We found the grey stone building hidden on a hill to the east of the town, and were sickened by what we saw. The building had broken or bricked-up windows; many of the rooms were dripping with water and their walls were smeared with faeces. Some smelt so bad I could only enter them holding my breath. The children inside were badly malnourished and near naked, often huddling in the darkness around the bare metal radiators for warmth. When we reached out to touch or comfort them, they instinctively flinched – such was their experience of physical contact. As I sat in the Land-Rover three days later, I was overcome with a delayed wave of shock about our visit, and I broke down in tears.

At the fellowship we held a number of special prayer meetings and decided we would try to do something about it. Everyone was so emotional about the situation. We sent out faxes to contacts we had in the UK, the US and Holland, and organized a team to lead some children's programmes there. I remember the shaven-headed children, so under-nurtured, struggling to sing even simple songs. Sometimes they would join in with hand gestures, and we counted that as something.

Churches responded over the next four months. A group came out from Holland to help reconstruct a section of the building. A couple of trucks came out from the UK with blankets, sheets, cots and beds. We felt that we were having some impact on the lives of the children there, but we soon discovered we were fighting an uphill battle against local corruption. Much of the aid was being stolen by the staff or other connected officials. Throughout the summer of 1992 and into the following year, we seemed to be constantly pouring aid into a black hole. When we returned a month after deliveries, half of it would have simply vanished. It seemed to me that there was almost a hidden policy of keeping it looking constantly in need of aid and pilfering what was sent. We tried to visit regularly to hold some accountability, but to make one step forward for the children was taking us ten hard strides. It was a heartbreaking situation, and the young members of our fellowship took it especially badly.

We cried out to God about it all. It seemed that what was needed was not an institutional orphanage, or one in the hands of a corrupt establishment, but a place run with a heart of love for the children. We kept our links with the orphanage, and also kept the issue in prayer.

From the remnants of the pre-war church, the Korçë fellowship had mushroomed into a 200-strong gathering during the course of the year – and the excitement there was huge. We had moved from our meeting place in the dusty Palace of Culture to the town library. Despite its buckling floorboards and smashed windows, it was still packed solid for the services. Our children's programme in the town puppet theatre had also drawn up to 500 a meeting. Sitting two to a seat, they would act out the hand gestures that *Teta* (auntie) Caralee taught them as their singing was heard streets away. We had also gained entrance to many schools to lead regular talks and question-and-answer sessions. Outside the town, Bible study groups had begun meeting regularly in Libonik, Progër, Dishnicë, Kamenica and around a dozen other places, and the numbers were growing weekly.

We were also regularly astonished by the ways in which God was using our work, either to add to our numbers or to make important connections for us. When Nikos, the border guard we'd met in the railway yard, had returned to his home village, most of his family and eight others there had come to the Lord as a result of his witness. One evening at the church, a middle-aged man with a shiny head presented himself to us as Dr Ilia, who practised in the village of Pirg. On the day that we had been stoned there, he had witnessed it happening and it had led him to seek us out. When we baptized him along with many others in the cold, clear waters of Lake Pogradec, Dr Ilia – and no one else – had risen up out of the water speaking in tongues, and he was as taken aback by it as the rest of us.

Through a friendship that developed that year, I was allowed access to a once secret and guarded document. The husband of Caralee's language tutor turned out to be the number-two officer in the Korçë secret police, the Sigurimi. One day, he invited me to his office for a coffee and 'to show me something'. Once a faithful Communist, the man had now lost his zeal for the system and was leaving for a simpler provincial police post. In a secure iron filing-room, he passed me a grey cardboard file bound with white tape and marked with the name 'Ian Paul Loring' on the front.

I fingered the cover reflectively. In it I saw the reports of the brown-suited spies who had followed us on our tour bus campaigns and their concerns that we had come to undermine their system. There was a report on the day we broke away from the tour in Tirana, and the man who, unfortunately for him, had been responsible for losing us. These things I had expected to see. What struck me most, though, were the details they had of my life in England: where I had lived, studied and worked. Did they have sources there? Had we let such things slip unwittingly in conversations? How had they come by such information? It was now just a matter of interest, for it no longer really mattered.

By the end of our first year in Albania, a huge number of individuals and Christian organizations had begun arriving in the country. Mike Brown, Caralee and I had now been joined in Korçë by Shirley Klippenstein, a curly-haired Canadian who helped us lead the church, and other missionaries and groups from the West were venturing out to help or pass through. These included both the good and the spurious, and we were to encounter them all.

One meeting I had was a particularly uncomfortable educa-tion. The leaders of a large US denomination came to visit us in our room in Little Paris one afternoon to discuss the Korçë church. The men wore black suits and were professional in their manner, and they each took one sugar in their lemon tea. Joseph, a gentle giant of a missionary from Florida, was with me, and our visitors sat in a neat row across from us. After a lit-tle small-talk, we waited for them to enlarge on their business.

'We hear that you guys have been doing a great job out here,' one man began.

'Thank you,' I replied.

'We'd, er ... we'd like to send out some of our denomina-tional missionaries to work with you ... three couples.'

Another man bent down to shine his shoe and glanced around our one-roomed home as he did so. 'You people are obviously very tired, and you need to raise some support,' he continued. 'Why don't you, Ian, your wife and some of your people here go on a tour of our churches in the States? I'm sure they will be very thankful, and show their generous support for this phenomenal work you've done.'

It was true that we were tired, and we did need some more support, but I was beginning to get the feel of this proposition.

'Yes,' chipped in the first man as he leant forward. 'After a year or so, you'd come away with enough to propel yourself into a new ministry in a different location out here. Our missionaries are all seminary graduates, ready to take the church here and its fledgling groups on to their next step.'

'Thank you for your interest in our work, gentlemen,' I replied, with a feeling of disgust rising inside. 'But I don't think this is the right location for your graduates.'

The men fell silent for a moment. The conversation resumed for a while, but it was awkward. As they left the room, I wondered if I had heard them right. My mission-field innocence felt suddenly tarnished. They had offered to buy out a piece of the Kingdom like some corporate acquisition. I felt strangely as if I had been here before, but it was an incident that left us all sick to our stomachs.

5 OVER THE EDGE TO ERSEKË

As the Land-Rover pulled our small party steadily higher into the snow-covered mountains south of Korçë on a bracing February day in 1993, I felt my stomach tighten and my blood begin to course quicker. We had been snaking up the bare hillside for around fifteen minutes, before the road hairpinned to the right and rose steadily over the crest of Qafë e Qarrit, Oak Tree Pass. We were about to enter what for us was completely new territory: Kolonja, the next state down from our home state. Ahead of us, a row of round gun bunkers spied out over the land ahead like the helmets of giant concrete soldiers. Beyond those, the hillocks rolled away to a crop of sharp mountain peaks rising perhaps 30 kilometres away. The view was spectacular and beautiful, stretching away to the most southerly parts of Albania. I felt a little as I imagined Joshua's men might have, spying out the Promised Land; our destination too had a reputation for being hostile and wild. We were driving to a meeting in the state's principal town, Ersekë. Our vehicle coasted over the far edge of the pass, and zigzagged down through the pine trees and oak shrubs.

For some time now, Caralee and I had been wondering what the next step in our work might be – and where. A growing team of foreign missionaries was heading up the Korçë church, and the Albanian leadership there was beginning to mature and come through. We had recently visited the US for a break, and while there I had heard a talk at Fuller Seminary in Pasadena that seemed to galvanize my thinking. The seminary's president had given a talk about the nature of change, and observed that all great change happened on the margins – at the edge. I had been asking myself this question: if Korçë had been the edge for us eighteen months earlier, where had the edge moved to now?

At the daily morning prayer meetings in our new apartment close to the football stadium, the possibility of an outreach to Ersekë had been raised repeatedly. We had discussed it with some close friends, a Dutch couple called Barth and Matilda Campanjen, who worked with a mission organization named Ancient World Outreach, and they confirmed that Kolonja was the only area of the country which to date had no Christian presence, neither church-plant nor humanitarian agency. Through them we also learnt a little more about an important figure from the region's past, an Albanian believer named Petro Nini Luarasi. He was a famous literary figure and educator, who before the war had written about how he longed to see Holy Communion taken in Ersekë. It all seemed to point us in the same direction: on the road over Qafë e Qarrit.

We had been waiting for the right time to go there. Our hope, if it were possible, was to build a bridge between the church in Korçë and the town, and begin a major work there. Not everyone in the fellowship, though, had been affirming about the idea. Some had expressed their reservations and concerns: Did we really want to work so far away from Korçë? Might it not be too big a step for us? Memorably, a little later a Scottish girl visiting the church told everyone of a vision she had had while praying about the matter. It was of a rose growing up and blossoming beautifully before being strangled by the thorns around it. 'It will grow and look nice, but then it will choke and die. That is what will happen if you start a work in Ersekë!' she announced authoritatively.

It was hard to simply dismiss the words of another believer as being wrong, and it had caused us a lot of soul-searching, but to me it didn't weigh up. I remember Xhaxhi Berti sitting on our settee, warily chewing her message over and then expressing my thoughts completely. 'How can sharing the gospel anywhere be wrong?' he had challenged her.

From the foot of Qafë e Qarrit that day, the car bounced along southwards through small villages of houses surrounded by unstable-looking stone walls, and over the wide, rocky riverbeds that swept down from our left. Occasionally Caralee braked to let cattle lumber off the road. An hour out of Korçë, as we crossed over a small bridge, a cluster of low apartment blocks appeared ahead of us on the road. To their left, the land swept up into a ridge of mountains shrouded in the heavy cloud base. We had arrived in Ersekë.

Caralee slowed along the main street to park the vehicle, and the people stood and looked at us with a coldness I could feel. As we walked across the main square, the wind was damp and whining through the TV aerials, and we were left in little further doubt as to how the residents felt about our presence here. People stepped forward and spat at the ground around us.

We met a number of town officials over the next couple of hours, including a thin-faced man in a brown suit whose name was Reshati. As head of the local education department, Reshati had heard about how we'd renovated the school in Progër, and we talked a little about possibilities in Ersekë. We also met the head of the local hospital, Dr Bendo, a man with eyebrows like an owl's, to discuss what medical aid they needed; he too knew of our deliveries to the hospital in Korçë. When the meetings were over, we drank tiny cups of thick, Turkish coffee with the two men at one of the few spartan cafés open, and we shook hands with them as we left. We had established our first tentative links in the town.

Over the following months we began to make regular visits to Ersekë. Initially we took along medical supplies and books for the high school, but soon we began to organize meetings in an austere building on the south side of the town known as the Kend i Kuq (the red corner). Mike Brown and I preached there, others from Korçë came along to share testimonies, and Caralee and our children's team began to hold small gatherings for the young. All the while, we kept praying.

With the exception of its small, well-kept parks, Ersekë was not an attractive place to look at, and even one of the parks had a gun bunker in it. The majority of its 7,000 residents lived in functional five-storey apartment blocks. The outside walls of these, if they weren't bare brickwork, were coated with a crumbling salmon pink or lime green plasterwork. In between, a number of older stone cottages were dotted around, their red roof tiles crumbling away almost to rubble. The town's unsurfaced dirt roads became a slough of brown mud when it rained, but the main ones were redeemed a little by the neat rows of pine trees along them. Around the edge of the town were clusters of ramshackle wooden outhouses where the brown hens and green-tailed cockerels competed with the local stray dogs and cats to scratch at the rubbish. Donkeys and shaggy, auburn-haired mules carried their owners in from the villages swinging their legs side-saddle; black-spotted pigs and horned cattle occasionally went about their own business trotting through the yards.

Though by this time the people of Korçë had begun to wear an assortment of the previous year's Western fashions shipped in as aid, that aid had not yet reached Ersekë. The clothing there was still the basic three-colour Communist issue, only even more worn out. There was a thick atmosphere of heaviness in the town. Those who had employment worked either at the hospital, the town hall or the army base; there was little private enterprise yet, except for the occasional man selling cigarettes from a crate on the street corner. The remaining majority lived on government assistance. In the town's dimly lit billiard halls, the men were drunk, and there were regular brawls between them and the surrounding villagers.

While most of the rest of Albania had tentatively embraced democracy the previous year, Ersekë remained defiantly hard-line Communist, and the mood of the people was one of real anger. They felt that their system had been betrayed, a system which they still believed in. There was even talk in the town of counter-revolution. Foreigners were seen as dirty and immoral, or as spies. To them we were the enemy, and that was made plain as the residents avoided us on our way to the Kend i Kuq, or stared coldly and spat.

We visited the town every week throughout the spring and talked further with Reshati about the school, and as we did so a plan began to formulate in my head. The motto of Open Air Campaigners is 'To present Christ by all means everywhere', and that was what I had decided we would do in Ersekë. We would base a campaign around the renovation of the town high school. It would be like the project we had undertaken at Progër, only much bigger. Progër was a village: Ersekë was a whole town that had never had the message of the gospel presented to it before. I wondered just how big we could make our invasion, for that was what it was going to be. To maximize the impact we needed to target all the different groups of the town – the pensioners, the adults, the teenagers and the children – with the best possible way of reaching them.

As the weather turned milder and we drove to and fro over Qafë e Qarrit, I felt the Lord was stimulating my mind with ideas. I decided we would call the campaign 'Project

Resurrection', as the goal behind it all was to bring a new church to life. I knew that in the process we must be prepared for the spiritual sparks to fly. At the church meetings in Korçë, we prayed and prepared for the project in earnest with a mid-July start date. I mapped out a detailed plan for each of the different teams we would need: to go door-to-door with Bibles, to lead programmes for the children and high-school students, to speak to the adults in the town, and to renovate the school building. I considered who could lead the teams, as the most mature Albanian believers were still only two faith-years old, and appealed to churches in Fresno and Bristol to send out people to help us – more than before, if they could. The antici-pation began to build week by week with increasing numbers stepping forward to volunteer.

In our Korçë Bible study at that time, as we prepared for the Ersekë project, two young men arrived alight with enthusiasm for God, and their story strengthened all our hearts. Two years earlier, around the time we had met Nikos the border guard in Thessaloniki, the men, Petrika and Vangjush, had been fleeing the country for Greece when they had stopped to sleep high in the border mountains in the ruins of an old Orthodox church. As they had contemplated their lives, they had cried out into the night sky: 'We have no future and our country is in a mess. If you are there, O God, then reveal yourself to us.'

Vangjush recounted with wonderment how, later that night, they had both seen a vision of a white-haired, fiery-eyed man wearing brilliant robes. The image was just like Christ the judge in the book of Revelation – a book that they had never read. The man in the vision had spoken to them: 'If you sin-cerely seek me, you will find me. Now go.' The young men had interpreted this to mean 'go to Greece', and the following day they had climbed over the ridges and down towards the railway lines of northern Greece.

For the next two years they had struggled as refugees, there and on the island of Rhodes, but had constantly visited different churches seeking further understanding of God. In a church in Rhodes Town, another experience drew them both to a moment of repentance and a fuller grasp of the gospel. They had then finally felt able to return to their families in Korçë, where sixteen more members were added to the fellowship as a result of their testimony over the following two weeks.

The day to begin Project Resurrection came quickly upon us, and on the first day of our three-week campaign we walked once more along the main street of Ersekë with the teams. Over forty had joined us from Korçë and the surrounding area, and thirty from England and the US. The town's people stood and regarded us coldly again as we made our way across the central square and past the post office, with its fading Soviet-style lettering, to a chicken restaurant on the town's southern fringe. We had been in and out for over four months now, but the hatred had not diminished. It had, if anything, intensified in relation to our numbers.

With a welcome from the education office at least, work on the high school got under way. The renovation needs at the building were as great as they had been at the village school in Progër. The inside walls were in dire need of a coat of paint, the wood stoves needed repairing and the outside walls replastering, and new doors needed to be hung throughout. Window glass was once again scarcely in evidence. The English and Americans worked alongside the Albanian believers, as well as craftspeople and labourers from the town, sharing their skills as they applied fresh coats of blue and white paint with long rollers and re-rendered the outside walls. I remember Niko, a man from Korçë who ran a business on the town's outskirts changing truck tyres with little more than brute strength, whipping the Albanian youth into shape and getting everyone singing and dancing as they worked.

A local boy named Koli soon became an additional member of our workforce. We noticed little Koli wandering barefoot in his matted goatskin vest, rummaging around the town's rubbish areas for food, often being kicked and mocked as he went. We learnt that he was essentially an orphan, as his father, a drunkard who lived in a nearby cowshed, was incapable of caring for him. We decided to adopt Koli for the project, and after being bathed and shaved to remove his lice infestations, he began to warm to everyone's attention and put his hand willingly to whatever needed doing. Koli would always call Caralee 'Adelina', and we assumed, because of his obvious learning difficulties, that this was a mispronunciation. A little while after the project, we helped to find Koli a place in the improved Korçë orphanage. There we discovered two of his long-lost sisters, and they were all reunited. One of them was called Adelina.

The door-to-door team began delivering a copy of the Bible up the stairwells of every apartment block and to every cottage, inviting people to a series of evening meetings in the school, where Mike Brown and I would be preaching. The children's and youth teams organized outdoor games on the school's dusty playing fields with hundreds in attendance. They ran huge competitions, with prizes, told Bible stories, preached sketchboard messages and taught the town's young to memorize verses of Scripture. One team visited the hospital to talk and leave literature with the patients.

Each day I seemed to be running around everywhere pumped up on adrenaline, doing a little of everything and meeting with the different leaders to keep tabs on how each front was progressing. As both the local and national media took an interest in the project, we were able to highlight some the region's Christian history in the life of Petro Nini Luarasi. Luarasi had originally established the school, and his statue still stood in its front yard.

It was becoming clear by the middle of the second week, however, that everyone's morale was taking a battering from a constant stream of little incidents. The water supplies had been turned off at our dormitories. When bread deliveries arrived they would be stale. People were being regularly overcharged for things they had bought in shops. The building materials were vanishing. Games equipment was being stolen. Drunks kept turning up at the meetings in the high school with the intention of causing trouble – and on and on. Every day there seemed to be something more. I sensed that it was crucial to the project's success to raise everyone's spirits. We had felt uncertain about preaching in the open air as there had been these incidents and open aggression in the streets towards us, but I decided that we needed to go on the counter-attack. Now was the moment to take our offensive right to the centre of Ersekë.

The next day we split into a number of small street teams, and after a briefing session set off to different places around the town. Caralee, Ilo the flautist, Iliri the huge ex-drunk and I made our way to the small fruit and vegetable market opposite a run-down building for military officers. We were all determined in our mission, but I was apprehensive as we erected our sketchboard. When I began to address those milling by, outlining a dollar sign in blue paint across the white paper, a group soon gathered around us, and we all got involved in conversations with people for over half an hour. It had gone well and we were encouraged. The next step was to do it right in the heart of the town.

We chose our site in front of the town's museum, with its grey metal mural of soldiers striding boldly forward to a glorious Communist victory. Across the square were the Socialist Party offices and the balcony where Enver Hoxha had once addressed the town. At the base of the apartment blocks to our left, the cafés were doing steady business as groups of men sat out around tables in the warm summer weather, drinking beer and raki.

As we slotted the sketchboard poles into the back of the board, the curious began wandering over in ones and twos. Caralee was going to preach, so Ilo, Iliri and I hung back around the edges of the gathering crowd with the intention of talking to those who seemed interested in the message. Groups of men sauntered over boisterously, calling to others outside the cafés to come and see what the commotion was. The sight of a crowd was drawing an even bigger number, with people running up to the rear ready for the sport of what might transpire.

I began to feel deeply apprehensive. I did not like the atmosphere. I glanced across at Iliri: he too looked worried. Caralee was suddenly boxed in. I could hear her voice as she began, but I couldn't quite see between the heads of those in front. We waited.

'*Gjepura!* That's rubbish!' someone shouted. 'Take your filthy lies with you back to America.'

'*Mbylle gojën*. Shut up, you old fool, and let her finish,' came another cry. I glanced around, trying to see a way through to her, but she was tightly surrounded.

Suddenly there seemed to be jostling at the front. I felt a sudden rush of panic. 'Caralee, are you okay?' I shouted. 'Caralee?' I heard no reply.

'Yes!' she answered finally, with a little shakiness in her voice.

I began to breathe a little more slowly. I continued to try to get a clear view through to the sketchboard, but I could just see her arm dabbing paint at the top of the paper. When her short presentation was over, the crowd began to break up. Iliri and I hastily wove our way forward. On either side of Caralee, standing like hired bodyguards, were two young men: a dark-skinned gypsy youth with a heavy frame, and a broad-shouldered lad who must have been over six feet tall.

Caralee looked a little shaken. 'The crowd just seemed to turn, Ian,' she explained. 'They were coming towards me, and these two men just stepped out in front of them.'

The youths introduced themselves as Elisi and Tero. I talked with them for a little while, and invited them along to the evening meetings. They said that they would be glad to come, and I sensed that the Lord had done something instantaneous in both their lives there in the square.

As the crowd drifted back towards the cafés, we dismantled the sketchboard and made our way to the high school. Later, as the other teams reported back, I felt as if there had been a clash with spiritual darkness on the streets. A little light had flashed into that darkness, and not the other way around. From now on, there was a noticeable lightening of spirit throughout the teams; even around the town, a softening of hostilities could be seen in people's faces and in the treatment we received from those we dealt with.

The door-to-door teams had worked so zealously around the *pallatet*, or apartment blocks, and cottages that they completed their task of delivering Bibles everywhere inside of ten days. With half the project time remaining, it seemed a good idea to send them round again to ask people what they thought about what they had read. Many contacts were made and conversations had, but one incident for me gave an unsettling insight into local folk-practices.

When I met Xhaxhi Berti one afternoon during the second week, he was worked up about a situation he'd become involved in. He explained that a little girl called Yllka had made a commitment to Christ during the children's programme and had then invited him and others to her house. There the girl's parents were terrified, claiming that, because of this, Yllka had betrayed the 'good spirits'. Berti had been back to reassure them and pray with them the previous evening, assuming they were succumbing to superstitious fears, but he had an uneasy look in his eyes.

'I saw three images, Ian, like shadows, sitting on the settee drinking coffee,' he said quietly. 'The father is saying that the "good spirits" are now going to come for their dues. They were hysterical,' he said, shaking his head. 'I asked them to throw out their shrine, but they wouldn't!'

'I'd like to come with you,' I replied. That evening, Berti and I, and another man from the American team, made our way up the unlit stairwell to Yllka's parents' apartment. Berti introduced us to the family. The 'good spirits' apparently came here every night demanding payments of tobacco and money. I had heard a little about this practice before, out in the villages, but was wary of taking it all at face value. Yet as we prayed with them about the situation, I felt the hairs on the back of my neck begin to rise, and I was overcome with a sensation that something was about to happen, as if watching the build-up to a climactic shock in a horror film.

It was the most eerie of experiences. What I could then plainly see were the indentations of three forms pressed into the family settee. I also witnessed the cups of coffee the mother had prepared for the spirits rising to and from the table. Berti could see shadowy forms. The father could apparently see the full apparitions and was crying, 'They want my boy, my boy ...' and burying his face in his hands. I understood from Berti that this was the compensation they were demanding for Yllka: his younger son was to be in some way promised to them! All the time, we kept praying fervently. The parents were wailing hysterically. It was a chilling situation.

Suddenly, Yllka, whose name translated as 'little star', jumped up from the floor, grabbed the family 'good spirits' shrine, and threw it out into the black night from the balcony of the apartment. The indentations on the couch disappeared, and the atmosphere in the room lightened. Berti visited them again during the project, and we understood that the 'good spirits' had ceased to pay their visits. Afterwards, I was left reflecting deeply on it all.

The evening meetings in the school gymnasium drew in the town's adults in large noisy crowds. The gym was slightly below ground level, and I remember the faces of the children and younger teenagers, who we'd had to exclude, pressed along the skylights, peering in at the proceedings below. The atmosphere in the dimly lit room was smoky, heated and boisterous. Those who came to the meetings were not always there to listen, and many came along to disrupt them as they had little else to do. One teenager, a wisecracking troublemaker in a leather jacket whose name I learnt was Bledi, had to be dragged out regularly – but Bledi was not to be a lost cause. Mike Brown and I preached nightly, and many faces were present there again and again. On the last evening of the project, I felt that it was time to be bolder. I delivered a talk based on the book of Ecclesiastes, challenging people to consider the final value of all the things they were striving to achieve with their lives.

'Is it chasing the wind?' I appealed. 'Stand up and be counted if you are prepared to make a choice of real value – a choice for Christ!' Over three-quarters of those in the room stood up, perhaps around two hundred people. It was a heartening response, but I tried to temper it with realism. The actual count of those who walked on and grew in the faith might not tally quite so highly.

When Christ had been building the foundations of the church, he specifically chose individuals aside from others who followed him and set them apart as his disciples. For the first time in our work in Albania, I felt that this was the way to proceed with the teenagers of Ersekë who responded. I asked the team leaders if they would pray for guidance and do this. Mark Stoscher, a Californian seminary student whose eyes always held one confidently, went ahead despite his reservations, and Bledi the wisecracker and Caralee's bodyguard's Tero and Elisi were among those who were chosen. The leader of the young women's groups felt the task was too difficult, but she helped arrange for them to continue to meet.

Ersekë high school had been massively transformed, and the Albanian workers took the British and Americans to a nearby village for a farewell celebration feast. The leader of the American team was presented with the honour of a sheep's head, browned and steaming and looking squarely at him from the plate. There was a flurry of anxious glances around the table, we were later told. How would the man deal with this situation without causing offence? To everyone's relief, he picked up his knife and fork and tucked in. He was only a first-generation American. His family had all been Basque farmers, and he was apparently quite used to eating a range of anatomical delicacies.

What was clear by the end of our three-week project was that the whole town had taken a step away from outright hostility to the message we were bringing. There was an acceptance at least of our presence here. As we walked along the route we had taken on the project's first day, past the Italianate town hall and the bars where the heavy drinkers gathered, there were many different expressions on the faces. Now, people walked across to greet us. There were people smiling and waving. Others were nodding their acknowledgement.

As we were transporting the British and American teams out of Albania to the airport at Thessaloniki, our Land-Rover broke down. High above the Greek town of Edhessa, the engine lost its power. We let it coast along for a while as we prayed, but it would not splutter back to life, and it drew to a slow standstill against an incline in the road. Everything was suddenly quiet. Below us Edhessa's apartment blocks seemed strikingly clean and white after Ersekë's. Through the passenger window the summer breeze was warm, and the nearby roadside fruit stalls were laden with heaps of blood-red cherries we could smell. It lifted our spirits a little as we waited for the breakdown services, but inside I had a sinking feeling. When the van arrived, our vehicle needed to be towed away. The engine had taken a hammering along the mountainous back-roads for eighteen months, and this was its final kilometre. We had to continue our journey by coach.

It was a few weeks later, as we took a short break at a friend's house in England, that the implications began to sink in more fully. It would be impossible to continue so much of our work in Albania without the vehicle. It was a crushing realization. I felt completely worn out from all the work on Project Resurrection. The teams had worked so hard at their tasks, day and night, and Caralee and I were now sleeping long hours through the day to recover. We gathered together all the money we had, but it wouldn't stretch to a replacement. We had been successful in pulling in support to fund the campaigns and projects, but we were personally still living on the breadline. I felt so depressed about the loss of the vehicle that I didn't even feel I could summon up the energy to write a prayer letter about it.

One evening, as we mulled over the future, we received a telephone call from Betsy Reeves, the woman who had organized the reunion of Caralee's travelling friends in Fresno. I talked with her for a while about how the project had gone and how we were feeling so demoralized about things. I tried to avoid mentioning the Land-Rover directly, but she sensed that I was talking in circles.

'Come on, Ian,' she probed. 'What is it? There's something that you're not telling me.'

'Well …' I hesitated. 'You know, Betsy, we've had a bit of a problem. The Land-Rover's gone to a better place.' I tried to make light of it, but inside I was moved to tears that someone had asked.

'I see,' she said. 'I guess that's a bit of a big one to replace, isn't it?'

'Too big,' I replied.

'Could you just hold the line there, Ian?'

For a minute or so, I could hear the muffled tones of a background conversation. Caralee was looking across quizzically. 'I don't know! She's talking to someone,' I whispered.

'Hi, Ian, you there?' Betsy began. 'Listen, I've got a group of people here with me right now. I've had a talk with them and we're all in agreement. We'd like to buy you a new one. What do you say?'

I was speechless and overcome with emotion. Within 48 hours of the conversation, the money had been wired to a Basingstoke Land-Rover dealer, and we selected a brand-new ex-display model. The impact it had on us was immense. To me it felt like God's gift to us for all the work we had put in – a prize and a foretaste of the coming Kingdom. It was as if God was saying to us: 'Keep going to the edge and you won't be left to fall over.'

6 MOUNTAIN PIONEERING

The cold autumn winds and heavy showers arrived in Korçë not long after we drove our brand new Land-Rover back from our rest in England. Not only did the season turn quickly, but the rapid changes in the life of the town since we had arrived at the beginning of 1992, a little under two years earlier, seemed ever more apparent. Many of those changes gave a superficial appearance of modernization – a Western icing on an old ex-Communist cake – but underneath things often remained decaying or dysfunctional. While some of the town's residents tuned their newly purchased satellite dishes to MTV, their neighbour's houses were crumbling away. As we struggled to find fresh vegetables and milk, boxes of Mars Bars and Snickers were stacked up in the shops. When foreign aid money had arrived, it had been spent on new trashcans and concrete paving flags while the electricity and water systems were near to the point of collapse.

Since the borders of the country had opened, along with an influx of new money brought by those returning home had come the rapid acquisition of electrical appliances. Fridges, cookers, heaters and even the deep-fat fryer arrived fresh out of their boxes – clean, white trophies of new wealth for the family home. As the demand on the electricity supply increased, however, fuses on the outside of apartment blocks in Korçë began to fizzle out. Most people did not replace the fuse, but twisted in a metal nail as a makeshift substitute. As this practice built up, it bounced the electricity supply back to the local transformer. When the metal wedges there blew out, the workers rammed in crowbars, and this then knocked the current back to the Korçë sub-station. One chilly day in early November, a huge boom echoed out across the entire town like the noise of a shell dropped from some passing bomber: the people of Korçë had blown their electricity station into the ether.

The lights went out and the fridges stopped humming. As each week passed, we hoped the sub-station might be repaired. Caralee and I lit our flat by candlelight, cooked using a small gas camping stove and kept ourselves warm wearing three layers of clothing: we had no other means of heating. It was a freezing cold winter, with temperatures falling regularly to minus ten degrees and below. Flu viruses were widespread, and we inevitably caught them. As bitterly unpleasant as it was, we washed our clothes by hand in cold water and bathed as best we could. There was also no bread to be had anywhere. The town was to be completely without electricity into the January of the following year.

We moved our church meetings forward into the daylight hours, and continued with regular follow-up work to Project Resurrection in Ersekë. A team of forty volunteers took a coach over Qafë e Qarrit every Friday afternoon. It soon became clear that many of those who had stood up at the meeting in the high school gym on the very last evening had not followed through. Perhaps for some people it was the desire to 'please the foreigner' that had made them stand, or for others the desire to add Christ to their existing gods, or any number of other reasons, but initially there were just seven adults meeting regularly together as a result of all the evangelistic work we had undertaken. It would have been easy to conclude at this point, using the 'prophetic word' shared, that the rose had hardly even sprouted from the soil, let alone blossomed.

The teenage boys' group, however, including those who had been chosen as 'disciples', was going from strength to strength, and the girls' group was maintaining its numbers. This I felt was a real vindication of the strategy God had led me to adopt. The Friday children's meetings in the military officers' club were also continuing to draw large crowds. As we went on visiting Ersekë, though, the numbers steadily began to increase again, as the youth who were strong in their convictions drew others back in and affected their friends and families. By Christmas time that year, 1993, over a hundred were in regular attendance.

We could say to ourselves with a sense of accomplishment that the project had indeed brought about a 'resurrection' among the apartment blocks and muddy streets of Ersekë. A new church had been born there! At our Christmas party in Korçë town library, the room was filled to capacity as believers from across the area gathered under one roof for the very first time. On that day, I figured there must be around five hundred people playing party games, including old Ligor, hopping around like a carefree child. It was exciting for everyone to witness the growth.

The cold, damp winter months without any heating in our apartment did not help my physical health. I had a terrible burning sore throat and it just grew worse and worse. I had little energy and found it hard to breathe, and I learnt that I had in fact developed bronchitis. To tackle it, I took three consecutive courses of antibiotics, but each time the symptoms knocked me back down again. I tried to keep working, helping with the leadership of the Korçë church, continuing with journeys to the outlying villages and overseeing the teams visiting

Ersekë, but I had also become burnt out with the intensity of the work we'd been doing. I reached a point at the end of December where I could manage little more than leading Bible studies at our apartment or preaching at the fellowship's Monday night meetings. When these were over, I would slump into a chair, or sprawl across the bed if I made it that far, and sleep for long hours through the daytime as well as solidly through the night. Caralee would bring me cups of tea and I would drink a little and reawaken to find them cold. Ligor and a group of others came to pray for me, gathering around and laying on their hands. I knew that they were worried. I just felt deeply exhausted.

One afternoon, I lay on the couch in the half-light of our living room as the hours came and went. I yanked the cushions under my head, twisted and repositioned them, and then pushed them to one side as I tried to get comfortable. My eyelids were heavy but my lungs felt deeply raw and painful. Sometimes I'd open my eyes and through a haze see Caralee's form moving around the kitchen, or I'd try to check the clock on the wall. I wasn't sure if I was awake or asleep when it began, but I sensed that God was speaking to me. I saw pictures of huts like army barracks close to a ridge of high hills. There were people meeting there, many faces that I knew, Albanians and Westerners, and they were worshipping and organizing together before preparing to leave. I then saw myself driving through the Albanian mountains between different towns, overseeing a number of teams.

I slipped back into sleep, and mid-evening awoke again and pushed myself upright. I rubbed my face for a while and Caralee gave me a mug of tea. I thought about what I had seen. The pictures were vivid and the impression they made on me strong. I recognized what God was prompting me to do. It was a call to a further campaign, and this one was to be even bigger than Project Resurrection – like it, but in a number of different places simultaneously. As I reflected on the dream, I sensed God saying: 'No matter how big the things you have done before, there is always more.' It felt like a further challenge to go back to the edge: a challenge not to settle and be satisfied.

My strength had recovered a little by the time we left for a break in the States in the January of 1994. I was conscious immediately that if the project were to crystallize by the summer months, the best time for such operations, it would be necessary to begin organizing the logistics right away. The call to this campaign had come with an intensity, and I now felt a driving urgency to make it all happen. I spoke at supporting churches in New Jersey, Alaska and California, and talked with an organization called Alongside Ministries about training and recruitment for the project. My plan was to begin with a foundational week where all those taking part could gather at a camp for teaching, worship and preparation. Teams would then separate to three or four different towns for a further two weeks, with a view to planting new churches or strengthening existing ones. The number of Albanian believers had now grown, and we had more volunteers and those who were maturing in their leadership abilities. I felt that we were ready as a growing movement for the next push on from Project Resurrection.

Back in Fresno once more, Betsy Reeves could see that my health was still very borderline. She and her husband insisted that they check me into a private clinic for a thorough examination while we rested at their summer house down near San Diego. The Reeves' had decorated their spacious French-chateau-style house along the theme of C.S. Lewis' Narnia stories: the way from the kitchen into a bedroom was through a large blue wardrobe! It was a wonderful place to relax in, delightful and interesting, but still comfortable. At the rear of the house, a large bay window gave views out over the deep blue Pacific as it swelled and rolled down on to the shore, gently hissing as it dragged over the grains of sand and tiny pebbles.

Late one afternoon, as I sat looking down on to the ocean, four dolphins played close to the water's edge. I watched as they swam along in close formation, rolled over and blew up small spurts of spray from their blowholes. I followed their movements for what was in fact an hour and a half, but it seemed to flash by in minutes. The creatures seemed so at ease luxuriating in the water and the rays of the Californian sun. Their presence so close to the house seemed to ease my thoughts and spirit, and I found myself conscious that I was receptive to God in a way that I had not had the space to be for many months. I felt as if my relationship were back to a level of his concern for me as his son. Like the dolphins in the water, I luxuriated in it for a while. It was a wonderful place to be.

I remembered a conversation I'd had with a seasoned missionary to the Balkans three years earlier, as I'd prepared to leave Bristol for Bulgaria with an aid truck. She'd been translating documents for the team and could tell by my demeanour I was in a hurry. 'Ian,' she'd said, looking at me squarely, 'the Lord is not going to stop the world spinning on its axis for you, but if you are quiet and spend time with him, he will show you how to get everything done in the time that is given.'

I'd taken the mild rebuke and the advice. Now I felt that God was reminding me of this truth again, and I began to feel far more at ease. Ever since I'd had the dream about the next campaign, I'd felt driven to work it all out; there were a million and one things to organize. With Project Resurrection I'd been able to keep my finger on the pulse; with the next campaign it would mean having the right leaders in all the planned locations. But now I felt I could rest in the knowledge that he would reveal how to get it all done and who I should draw into leadership for each of the teams. I continued to watch the dolphins until they slipped out of view.

At one of the most efficient and high-tech clinics I've ever seen, the doctors diagnosed my health as being in a worse condition than I realized. I was told that I had in fact had walking pneumonia for eighteen months. There was scarring inside my lungs, one of which was three-quarters full with fluid and the other half full. The doctor gave me a course of antibiotics and Prednisone, which eventually worked but gave me a whole range of peculiar side effects as they cleared the fluid up. With the Lord's help, though, by the end of our stay at the Reeves' house I felt that I knew who almost all of the team leaders were going to be.

Once we had flown back to Albania, I resumed preparations for the campaign in earnest. I soon discovered a location in Voskopoje, a village high in the mountains west of Korçë that had once been home to an Orthodox monastery. The place was ideal for the format I had envisaged: a week's preparation together at a camp, before groups fanned out to different locations for a further two weeks' outreach and evangelism. The site itself had been a training centre for the Pioneers, the Communist youth movement, and had several buildings and stone huts surrounded by pinewoods. The buildings were in a typically run-down condition, but I figured they could be made fit for habitation again with a little preparation. The location was beautiful, with fresh mountain air and the fragrance of the trees – and it felt right. It was a camp so like the one I had seen as I'd dreamt of the project on our apartment couch. From then on, I christened the campaign 'Project Voskopoje'.

At meetings in our living room, we prayed every day for the project. I liaised with Alongside Ministries and our contact churches in the US. I appointed those Albanians who would lead different teams – the children's, teenage and adult programmes – and encouraged them to begin their own preparations.

However, just as it was with Project Resurrection and the questionable prophetic word about the rose strangled by thorns, there were issues once again that made the way forward more of a battle than a smooth progression. This time it was difficulties surrounding the Albanian leaders I'd chosen. Some believers were jealous of those selected. The leaders themselves rubbed each other up the wrong way as they jockeyed for position and superiority, arguing like the disciples on the road to Jerusalem about who was the greatest. It was with a certain frustration that I had to spend a lot of time and energy helping everyone involved sort out their differences.

In the weeks running up to Project Voskopoje, Reshati, the brown-suited Director of Education in Ersekë who had helped open the way for Project Resurrection, visited us regularly at our Korçë apartment. As we became friendlier with Reshati, he felt able to let us in on a problem he'd been suffering with for eleven long years.

'I have these headaches,' he explained to me one evening, glancing around the room uncertainly. 'Sometimes it feels as if a metal pole is being rammed down into my head.'

We learnt that he came from a Bektashijan Moslem family, a folk-religion that mixes ancestor worship, witchcraft and Islam and which is widespread in the region despite so many years of atheistic Communism. He explained that a relative had put a curse on his family, and that he and his two brothers suffered the same debilitating head pains. Reshati had travelled to many of the region's Bektashijan shrines, or *teqes*, to seek remedies from the priests or *babaijt*. He had a number of strange concoctions that used locks of his own hair, and sought relief by placing pieces of the Koran stitched into material in his armpits. They had not brought him any lasting relief.

As we talked with Reshati, I told him that if he wanted the healing work of Christ it would be necessary to denounce his involvement in Bektashijan Islam. I sensed that he was willing.

One clear spring day, he took me to a *teqe* high in the mountains south of Korçë. Way below I could see the pine trees and the valley floor with its river glinting over a white rocky bed. As we entered a little garden, the small hexagonal building had an air of death around it. The *babaijt* interceded to their god via the previous dead *babaijt*, whose bodies were housed inside. Reshati renounced the curse in the presence of the *baba*, who stood impassively in his cream robe and green fez. He replied by issuing warnings of the curse's power. I was just glad to be out of the place.

One evening, not long after, Caralee and I and a Dutch couple visiting us prayed for Reshati for over two hours. It was an intense evening, but Reshati wanted the Lord to deliver him and he'd made his mind up to follow him. When we saw him again, his headaches were no longer troubling him. My experiences with both Yllka and the 'good spirits' and then with Reshati's curse made me reappraise my thinking about such matters. There was in my mind clearly more to both of these incidents than mere folk superstition.

As the start date for Project Voskopoje drew closer, the organizational activity intensified more and more, and at times I felt on the edge of panic. We had teams coming in to work with us from England, Scotland, Alaska, California and France, totalling 60 people, and alongside these 150 Albanians were preparing to work. The logistics of how we were going to transport enough food and water to the site for them all, 25 kilometres up a poorly surfaced mountain road, was proving a further test. Obtaining final clearance to use the site had also become a complex matter. Like all land in Albania, the government had formerly owned it. Now, a number of different private parties were disputing its ownership.

While the matter dragged on, I made arrangements to collect several thousand Bibles from a warehouse outside Tirana for the teams to give out around the towns and villages. I prepared the agendas for the on-site teaching and worship services and helped the Albanian leaders prepare for their own locations. I was on a knife-edge about it all, and I kept trying to remind myself of God's reassurance to me in the bay window of the beach house: 'I'll show you how to get everything done in the time that is given.' And so it was, just 48 hours before the overseas teams arrived in Albania, that we finally obtained clearance to use the former Pioneer campsite.

On the first day, as the convoy of coaches churned up the summer dust along the dirt mountain track as they edged their way slowly to the Voskopoje site, I was a little anxious about everyone's safety. Ahead of us was an old red Chinese truck with a trailer piled unfeasibly high with a loose heap of hay. The hay glared brilliant yellow in the summer heat. I glanced away over at the pinewoods, and the scent blew in through the open bus window. The heat waves were shimmering off the rocks around us. My eyes wandered back to the truck. With a sudden flash, the hay on the trailer combusted into an orange fireball that rose high above the stack. Everyone at the front of the coach gasped at the sight. The driver braked. The tractor began to veer to the edge of the road. Its left-hand wheels dropped over the edge and it began to tip. The driver jumped clear, tumbling back on to the track ahead of the coach. The whole flaming rig then toppled over the edge and bounced away down the mountainside. The site was horrifying.

The coach doors hissed open and we ran out to see if the tractor driver was okay. The man seemed shaken but physically fine. He was, however, inconsolable as he held his face in his hands. Most of his means of livelihood was now a smouldering wreckage below us.

We were shaken up by what we had witnessed, but our nerves eased a little over the first 24 hours and we settled into the camp. The rhythm of teaching and training sessions, sandwiched by worship services, led to the week passing swiftly by. In between our preparations, we had mass pine-cone fights in the woods, and rooted for our chosen nations as news from the World Cup was passed around. The outdoor games and the buzz in the kitchen cooking huge trays of stuffed peppers helped build team spirit and bond the many nationalities together. The camp format proved to be a good springboard for the mission, and had, I felt, been worth all the logistical anguish.

Teams set out from Voskopoje at the end of the week to work in five different locations. In Korçë and Ersekë the goal was to strengthen the existing churches and conduct evangelism in the many surrounding villages while assessing the most promising places for follow-up. From the town of Maliq north towards Lake Pogradec a similar strategy was being pursued. In two more places, Bilisht and Pojan, east along the road to Kapshtice border crossing, teams were heading to work intensively with the aim of planting two new churches. Once again, volunteers were going to visit door-to-door in the towns and villages, give out Bibles, preach using sketchboard messages, perform dramas, tell stories and organize games for the children.

Over the next two weeks, I bounced around the roads in the Land-Rover between each of the places, helping to solve problems and difficulties with the team leaders as they invited me. On Project Resurrection I'd put my hand to a little of everything in the field; now, I was operating in a 'hands-off' manner to enable the Albanian leadership to grow. For me, in one key way the campaign was more difficult than the previous ones. I

was leading it one step back from the front line, being everywhere and nowhere, removed from the pleasure of seeing the
fruit of God's work at close hand — until the final evening.

As word had filtered through from the team leaders, it had
become clear that to bring everyone together at the end we
would need a location far bigger than our meeting room. We
settled on the officers' club, close to our first room in Little
Paris: the meeting place and private bar of the town's military
officers and one of the last bastions of the old guard in the
town.

As the teams and those who had made commitments over
the two weeks arrived and took seats, the place began to fill up.
Groups of people milled about excitedly, shouting and looking
around at each other in curiosity, and surveying the building's
interior with its imitation marble tiles and broken windows.
The numbers arriving continued to flow in. The balcony was
soon packed. In the lower seating area all seats were taken;
others lined the walls around the edges, and sat in rows cross-
legged on the floor at the front. These were people that I had
not seen before: young Albanian men with thick curly brown
locks, children in colourfully jumbled clothing and middle-
aged women with their headscarves tied on tightly. I was
amazed. They were all here as a result of the campaign —
perhaps a further 400. I felt choked up. 'Thank you Lord,' I
whispered under my breath.

As the meeting got under way, the volume of everyone
singing together must have been audible across Little Paris.
When the time came for me to preach a message, I could feel
myself shivering about it. I had decided to make an invitation
to the Albanian workers. I wanted to challenge them to think
about taking a further step – a step into a year of full-time ministry to use whatever their giftings were: as evangelists, pastors
or children's workers. To take such a road would mean living by

faith as individuals and trusting in God for financial provision. Such a route was a challenge to any Western Christian, but the concept was totally alien to the Albanian mindset after decades of state provision.

I was afraid that in taking such a step, I would be left standing alone in the room with the cold wind of incomprehension blowing around me. But I felt that the time was right now to do it. I spoke for a while about God's faithfulness and the way he had provided for Caralee and me as we had begun working in Albania, with our Land-Rover and during the incident with the customs colonel. I concluded with a reference to the parable of the sower.

'The workers are few, yet the fields are white here for the harvest,' I appealed. The room was quiet and a little clammy in the evening heat. 'If you are ready to commit yourself to a year for the growing Albanian church, then come forward now and we will pray with you.' I sat back down, looking at my lap to avoid the gaze of the hall. My palms were wet with moisture.

For a long thirty seconds no one moved. Then there was the noise of chairs shuffling on the hall floor. Over the next couple of minutes, a group of people walked forward, each with a sense of almost ceremonial pride. I felt a little relief, but more a deep sense of the moment. Ten people had taken the step, including Holger and Iliri. There was also a young woman called Angela, a children's worker whose inner strength always shone through her sad eyes and who had taken her first copy of the Bible in the crowds at the football stadium three years earlier.

Their coming to the front of the officers' club was a milestone. I felt a lump in my throat and I couldn't help but reflect on it all. Albanian believers were growing up in their faith and moving forward into the leadership of their own church after just three years. In our first project at the school in Progër, they had formed the minority of the workforce; on Project Voskopoje they had been the majority by far. After I had asked one young man to sit back down and finish his schooling first, we formed huddles around each of the remaining nine, laid our hands upon them, and prayed fervently for their futures.

The project as a whole had been a success. Churches were already established in Korçë, Libonik and Ersekë, and Bible study groups were running in Mollas, Dishnicë, Progër, Kamenica and way south in the town of Leskovik. The three-week campaign, though, had seen new churches planted in Bilisht and Pojan, and the church that Holger was leading in Libonik had planted two more daughter churches in nearby villages. The number of believers in the southeast of Albania had doubled as a result of the campaign, and I felt tremendously satisfied with the summer's work.

It was less than a month later that a further team joined us in Albania from Pascack Bible Church in New Jersey. They had come to work with us to the south of Qafë e Qarrit in the town of Ersekë once more. The youth group in the town, including the young 'disciples', had grown through taking part in Project Voskopoje, and we set about consolidating our work there strengthening the newly born church. For me, as we undertook village evangelism again, it was a chance to work back alongside the regular people instead of with leadership teams, and I was happy for the time. It was refreshingly good fun.

During those days, a group of the town's youth asked Caralee and me if we would come to live in Ersekë. For a good while now, we had been asking ourselves where the next 'edge' for our work would be. The Albanian leadership in Korçë was maturing, and a number of new foreign missionaries had arrived to support Mike Brown and Shirley Klippenstein with all that was continuing there. We had thought about moving to one of the new church plants and had hoped that it might be Ersekë. It was clear to me that if the church there was to strengthen further, they would need a permanent presence with them, not just a visiting team from Korçë. With the boys' invitation, our minds were now made up.

As we prepared ourselves to leave Korçë and told others of our plans over the following month, an event took place in the life of the church which moved us all deeply with its unexpected consequences. For almost a year, Lola, a softly spoken woman with long brown hair, had been fighting cancer of the womb. Many people had visited her in the hospital; Shirley had been to her bedside almost every day. We had all been praying desperately that Lola would be cured, but suddenly she died. The church went into shock. God had answered so many of our prayers until now. Only months earlier we had seen another young woman in the church make a complete recovery from encephalitis after being in a coma for 36 hours – as a result of prayer, we knew. People were asking, 'Why not Lola? Her three children are now left without a mother!' It was difficult to find the words of explanation.

As it was, local belief held that a deceased person's spirit would roam their house, departing to its eternal destination only on the third day. During this time, it was customary for relatives to visit the house and grieve. Before she passed away, Lola had let it be known that she hated this custom, and I was asked if I would lead her funeral service the day after her death. As I prepared, I felt led by the Lord to preach a message based on the words Christ spoke to the thief on the cross: 'Today, you will be with me in paradise.'

In the vast Korçë graveyard, where row after row of headstones lined up to the surrounding pine trees, several hundred people were present. Her daughters and husband tossed handfuls of soil down on to Lola's coffin. There were many tears, including my own, and I spoke briefly.

'We can be sure, right now as we gather here, that Lola is already with her Saviour,' I concluded. 'Jesus reassured the thief as he hung dying at his side that not tomorrow but "today" you will be with me in paradise.'

The words were a direct challenge to the beliefs of many gathered there, and their effect sent waves through the crowd. When the service was over and we made our way from the grave, Holger, Shirley, Xhaxhi Berti and I were overwhelmed with the number of people who wanted explanations of this.

'How can you be so sure that Lola's soul is immediately in paradise?' one man asked me, holding on to the sleeve of my jacket.

I spent hours talking to Lola's relatives, and dozens of people were challenged to consider Christ that day. Many even became believers as a result. There are questions about God's purposes that are hard to answer, but one thing was for certain: Lola had brought more people to Christ in her death than many people do in their lifetimes.

7 MY QUEEN OF ARMENIA

Leaving the church in Korçë was an emotional moment for Caralee and me. We had seen it grow, from the handful of elderly men we had met in the town's back-streets on our first journey into the country, to a fellowship filling out a hired room at the library three years later. The wrench I felt about leaving was like letting go of a young loved one. We had been there at its re-birth; we had watched it take its first steps; and now it was growing up. Ilo the flautist, Iliri and Xhaxhi Berti were all present at a special communion service at the home of another believer to wish us farewell. Many people asked us not to leave, but we knew that it was right that we should. I had tears in my eyes as I shook people's hands and hugged them. It had been agreed that I remain an elder there, so I was not to be without contact, and I was deeply glad about that.

We moved into our new apartment in Ersekë in the October of 1994, buying it from the parents of a girl in our children's group. The whole process was thankfully swift and trouble-free. Our new home was up a dark stairwell on the second floor of a small concrete block of apartments at the southern edge of the town. It had a living room with an attached kitchenette, two medium-sized bedrooms and a toilet, and though it smelt a little damp it was perfect for our needs. Just as in Korçë, the water came on twice a day for a couple of hours, and the electricity supply cut out with a reliable regularity. The view from the living-room window faced west over the crumbling roofs of stone cottages towards a small pinewood and the same ridge of distant peaks that could be seen from the top of Qafë e Qarrit. While we had taken a short break in the US, the young men in the youth group had pitched up with their brushes and rollers and painted the walls, doors and window-frames a clean pale blue. It was a refreshing change from the salmon pink and pale green that wore you out with its ubiquity. We had learnt that the name Ersekë meant 'dry air': through the gaps in the ill-fitting window frames we could certainly feel the air, wet or dry.

From our first weeks in Ersekë, our apartment became a much-frequented visiting place for the young believers in the town, and we were glad to have it that way. Often they would drop by to play games or just to hang out, to ask us questions of faith or to share their problems with us. Some of the youth, including Caralee's 'bodyguards' and Bledi the wisecracker, seemed to be virtually living with us. Our new stream of visitors began a little after breakfast and continued until late in the evening. Regularly, there would be over thirty people in the house at once, with two rooms in use at the same time. I remember Bible studies numbering thirty-five in one room, with circles of people squashed inside. On other occasions, we organized tournaments of 'Killer Uno', playing with four decks of cards at once for prizes and silly punishments. The shouting and screaming in the bedroom as the cards were flung down passionately was at fever pitch.

We learnt to remember individuals by the quantity of sugar they took in their teas and coffees. Three spoonfuls was normal in the town, but one young man, a confident youth named Nachi with round wire-framed glasses, surpassed everyone with his taste for five. We were working our way through kilos of sugar every day.

Our living room became a major focal point for the developing life of the church. Mark Stoscher, the Californian seminary student who had chosen the young 'disciples' during Project Resurrection, had since graduated and felt called to Albania himself. He and his wife Ruth had decided to come and work alongside us to build the church in the town, and their apartment, close to the Kolonja state police station, was as busy with visitors as ours. We became like a family, joking and laughing together to help ease the problems and pressures.

As pastoral figures in the church, the young believers and others brought us all the difficulties and struggles of life, as well as deep questions of faith and confessions of their sins. Often, hours would pass simply talking to people about the Lord and his teachings, and pointing them to his guidance and example. One young man had lost his father only recently, and as the eldest of three brothers he was carrying all the weight of responsibility for the family at only 12 years old. It was the deepest relief to him to discover how God was there in real ways as his new and loving heavenly father. Another young man turned up on our doorstep, his forehead wrinkled with heavy lines, clutching his teacher's brown handbag. He had stolen it and then suffered an attack of guilt. With a little encouragement from us, he built up the courage to return it and face the consequences. There were others struggling with the pain and guilt of living with physically and emotionally abusive parents, with family pressures to become economic refugees in Greece, and with romantic failures – a huge thing in the changing culture.

On top of their own concerns, the youth had to deal with being teased by others in the town, including their families, for their faith. Always there was a ceaseless whispering pressure being brought to bear on new believers. 'Those foreigners are spies', 'They'll end up getting you killed', 'You'll wind up in prison', 'If you read the Bible, it'll turn you into an idiot', and on and on. But behind the common propaganda, there were others in the town who were more seriously opposed to the presence of the church.

From our earliest days visiting Ersekë, finding places to hold our meetings had been a struggle. Door after door had been closed in our faces, and always there were hitches and problems with the venues that did allow us access. Those who held the keys would then regularly 'forget' to turn up, and our workers would be left waiting outside. New property owners would cease old arrangements. Sometimes people made false accusations of non-payment. The landlords too had pressure put upon them by the town's hard-line Communists. It was all a deeply frustrating situation.

We had been holding our children's meetings through the winter in Ersekë's military officers' club, a rundown building with little window glass and badly broken floorboards. For three weeks in a row, the leaders had been locked out, but they had nevertheless persevered with the meetings in the front yard. One morning I arrived to see the children's leaders huddled together with a group of young people on the snow-covered ground. The temperature was well below zero. One of the teenage leaders had only a short skirt to wear, and her legs were turning blue. The children's hands were white with the cold. I felt a deep sense of anger at the sight. They were caught at the sharp end of some hard-liner's intransigence, and I felt I just couldn't let the situation continue.

Back at our apartment, I held an impromptu prayer meeting with Angela and some of our other children's workers. We sat on the edge of our living-room settee and I put my head in my hands. I felt so angry at the sight of the children in the snow.

'Lord,' I prayed, 'You know that we have managed up to now without buildings of our own. Well, I think we could really use one here in Ersekë!' The prayer was repeated around the room: everyone else had reached the same point of frustration.

Later in the week, I wrote a prayer letter to our supporters in the UK and the US explaining the problems we were having in the town and urging them to pray with us. We continued to hold the meetings inside and outside the officers' club over the following months, but it shortly became apparent that Pascack Bible Church in New Jersey, who had worked with us in Ersekë after Project Voskopoje, had decided they wanted to help us. They offered to work to raise nothing less than all the financial support we needed to make the idea possible. I was humbled by their generosity, and awed by God's provision.

Word quickly travelled around the town that we were looking to purchase a property, and there was many a knock on our apartment door from people offering to sell us everything from a barn to an apartment. Our search for a permanent base for the town's believers began, and we set our sights on a large stone building next to the town's police station which was being used by both the military and some village squatters. It seemed to show tremendous promise. Over the following month, however, the possibility of buying it swung backwards and forwards, with promises being made and broken by its owners. On the day we had set with them to meet certain requirements before purchase, the whole deal fell through and we were left feeling disillusioned. We'd really thought God was leading us that way. He was, however, opening another door for us, and the view on the other side was far better.

The following day, Niko, our Albanian language tutor, a man with handsome side-burns and little on top, informed us that his cousin was selling his house. As I walked around the property with Niko for the first time, I felt real peace about the place. The house was a two-storey building set alone in a small amount of land with six different fruit trees sprouting into blossom. To the east, beyond the surrounding rock wall, was a clear view across the fields and rows of gun bunkers to the 7,000-foot peak of Mount Gramoz. The snow-capped summit was brilliant white under the blue spring skies and the day felt fresh with a new beginning. I could see that the building would need a lot of work, but its potential was all there. We prayed about the move with Mark and Ruth and the church's baptized believers, and they too felt positive about the place.

As we pressed ahead, the dealings were all orderly and up front. The price that was settled on was exactly the amount we had been given by the New Jersey church. It all fitted.

We closed the deal at the end of May, and the work of converting the building to serve the needs of the believers began. The task of adapting Niko's cousin's old house became the focus of almost all of my energies and the centre of the life of our community for the next three months. The roof needed rebuilding and re-tiling, and all but the load-bearing walls needed knocking out to create bigger spaces. The floorboards, doors and windows all needed replacing, as well as a host of other tasks, but after renovating the schools in Progër and Ersekë we were becoming increasingly expert at this kind of thing! We also decided to lay down a concrete volleyball court at the rear; we knew that for the youth it would prove a popular addition.

Everyone lent a hand with the work that needed doing. Though we hired a group of builders from the town, the church's youth group did most of the physical labour. I remember two young men walking hours every day along the track from their village just to help us hump bricks and timber around. Even young children were turning up to carry shovels full of sand or to drag a wheelbarrow through the mud together. During the day there was much singing and laughing as everyone mucked in together, and at night the young men slept on site to guard the building materials from local thieves. We all shared a pride in building our own centre for worship. I felt a further source of pride: we were building the first new evangelical church in Albania since before the Second World War.

During the building work, I had to be constantly watching our materials suppliers and kept one eye on our engineer – the sweetest of guys, but regularly drunk. I learnt, oddly enough, that sand and cement were measured by the 'bunker' in Albania. There had been millions of gun bunkers covering the landscape for so many years that everyone knew their proportions all too well. If I ordered two bunkers of sand, though, one would be delivered, and if I didn't argue about that, half a bunker would be delivered the next time. Also, if I didn't watch the hired builders, they would thin down the cement mixture with more sand. The attitude was that as a foreigner I wouldn't know the difference. Such tactics were par for the course when working for 'institutional' employers, which was why many of the buildings in town were literally crumbling away. It was a tiring mentality to have to deal with; I couldn't take my eyes away from the site for a minute.

Because of the underlying hostility of many in the town, we used our land to meet and hold services from the moment we acquired it. Over a number of Sundays, while worship was in progress, I remember looking up through the rafters at the passing clouds in the open blue sky. Such matters just seemed like finishing details; we were so happy to have a place we knew we could not be locked out of any more. This was, of course, much to the chagrin of our opponents, and they began to turn the screws on us in every way they could. It was hard to witness our young people upset and bewildered by the marks they were achieving in school. We knew that some of them were being purposely marked down and flunked for their faith. It was also frustrating to hear the ridiculous gossip they spread to try to tarnish us: that I was a spy of the British government, that

Caralee and I were not married, and on and on. The Communists knew now that we would be harder to oust, and the tension began to increase.

With the development of our new church building, the numbers hanging out in our living room eased, though we still needed kilos of sugar. There were many new believers for us and the Stoschers to pastor and disciple. Such work had an intensity about it, but being at the heart of a close community I witnessed the fruits of it all, too – and I was satisfied.

Niko our language teacher, whose cousin had sold us the house, had attended our services on and off since the beginning of the year. Somehow, though, he hadn't quite grasped it all fully with his heart. A serious man by temperament, Niko regularly seemed to be following the kerb with his eyes as he went about his daily business. As the year neared its end, it happened that I asked him if he'd translate a number of chapters from a book about the pilgrim church. I needed it to teach a session at a Bible school we had started in Korçë for the Albanian leaders. I left the book with Niko before Caralee and I took a break in the US, and when we returned Niko was a changed man. No longer was he dourly looking at the ground: he was smiling and his whole bearing was lighter. Furthermore, he kept hugging me and calling me 'brother'. It was wonderful to see. Through translating the book, Niko had finally got it. He sat me down privately at the church.

'Ian,' he said with characteristic gravitas, 'I would like to be baptized.'

'We can do that, Niko,' I replied.

'Ian,' he continued, his eyes flitting around cautiously in case anyone might be listening, 'are you sure that everyone else here is saved?' I knew where he was coming from.

'Well,' I whispered back, 'I think that some of them are like you used to be.'

He thought about it for a moment. Then I saw a sparkle in his eyes. God had finally reached Niko through his love of history.

From the earliest days of our youth meetings in Ersekë, a teenage gypsy girl named Vito had been a part of our church family. With her shoulder-length dark hair and big brown eyes, Vito was a special favourite among our youth workers. We had learnt that she was in fact another sister of Koli, the orphan we had found living on the town's trash pickings during Project Resurrection. One day she was no longer present in the meetings. People began to ask, 'Where's Vito gone? Has something happened to her?' Soon a shocking story emerged. Around the time that she vanished, a group of men from the coastal town of Vlorë had been through Ersekë, asking for young boys and girls without any close family attachments and saying they were willing to pay for them. It was rumoured the children were to be used in an unthinkable trade for body organs being trafficked out of the Albanian port for the Far East. When the people of Ersekë found out that Vito had been sold to the men by her guardian, he had to flee for his life. The local police took up the matter but were unable to track her down. The church was devastated. I kept asking myself if I might not somehow have prevented it from happening. We wept together for Vito, and cried out to the Lord for her life.

Seven months went by and we heard nothing. Then one nippy spring day she walked calmly back into the church building wrapped up in a neat furry jacket. Everyone stopped what they were doing and stared at her. 'Vito,' someone gasped. We raced to gather around her. There were tears and laughter. People stared at her and stroked her on the arm just to check she was real. Her hair was shorter now, and auburn. The youth workers held her, and she held them. Everyone was asking the same questions: 'Vito, are you okay? Where have you been? What happened to you?'

The story now emerged. All those months ago, Vito had indeed been taken to Vlorë by the gang, and kept locked up in a squalid room full of other girls. The day before she was due to be shipped out, she had made her bid for freedom by squeezing her body out through a small window in the toilet. As she had been pursued by her captors along the Vlorë harbour front, a young man in a motor boat had pulled her on board and sped her away to safety on a peninsula of land across the water. Vito was now wearing a wide smile across her cheeky face and a ring on her finger. She and her motor-boat saviour had fallen in love and were now engaged! She had returned to let us all know that she was fine. We marvelled at her tale, and thanked God for the amazing way he had answered our prayers.

As the May 1996 Albanian general election approached, many people were fearful that after four years in the wings, under the guise of the reformed Socialist opposition, the Communists might somehow return to power. The governing Democratic Party, led by Sali Berisha, looked strong enough, but the faintest prospect for many who had suffered long under the old regime was enough to send them into a paralysis of fear. Kela was a 17-year-old, doe-eyed girl in the drama group of Ersekë church. During the Communists' rule, a relative had been sent by the government on a trip to France, and he had not returned as he should. As a consequence, Kela's family had been banished to live in a remote village in a dwelling that was little more than a barn. Kela began to visit Caralee and me regularly in the run-up to the elections. Often she would sit and weep on our settee, her slight brown arms shaking, and ask us to pray that the Democratic Party would win. The idea that her family might be sent back to the barn was tormenting her.

We counselled her that it was not so likely. We held her and encouraged her to draw on God's strength.

As it was, on the day of the election count in Ersekë, Reshati, now leader of the local Democrats, knocked on the door of our apartment. He had a heavy look of concern in his eyes as he stepped into the hall. He explained that they had caught one of the town's Communists stuffing papers into a ballot box. Some of Reshati's colleagues were insisting that an example be made of this man – that he either be beaten or shot.

'Jani, tell them what the West will think of them later, if they do this. They will listen to you,' he appealed.

I was with Reshati that to do such a thing was clearly wrong, but I did not want to get involved in local politics. It was an awkward decision; I prayed for the Lord's help. 'Okay, I'll come,' I replied, and I nervously put on my jacket.

At the Democratic Party office, I was explaining my thoughts on the matter to help Reshati out when suddenly there was a rapid cracking of automatic gunfire. Those in the room flinched and began to duck. Someone shouted: '*Ulu, poshtë!* Get down, everybody, get down!'

I fell to the floor. My heart was banging at my rib cage. The 'tat-tat-tat-tat-tat' of gunfire broke out again. A couple of bullets skimmed across the ceiling, punching holes in the wall above. I could hear the rest of the bullets smashing the building's roof tiles, which tumbled down on to the ceiling above, knocking chunks of plasterboard down on us. I quickly shuffled across the floor on my stomach to shelter under a table.

The shooting stopped. I heard a car screech off and accelerate away. The room was quiet and heavy with dust. Reshati looked across at me from the floor and shook his head. I was shaken but unhurt. As we got to our feet, the Socialists were being angrily cursed. I did not wait around in the office. Later that day, I heard that the Socialist Party office in Ersekë had been sprayed with bullets as counter-intimidation. Political tension had been ratcheted up in the town.

Across the country, both parties were doing their utmost to ensure their side triumphed, with grass-roots activists using dirty tricks and tactics that were undermining democracy. It had been clear to many people that the Democratic Party had the majority of national support, but when the ballot papers were counted and they polled over-high results and victories in some towns that were obviously Communist strongholds, a smell of corruption and malaise was left hanging in the country's air.

A little more than three weeks after election day, Angela told us over dinner that a little wavy-haired boy in our church, also named Bledi, was ill. Bledi was examined in the town hospital on suspicion of appendicitis, but there Dr Bendo discovered a cancerous tumour the size of three apples. He explained to us rapidly that Bledi's tumour was already touching some of his other organs. Angela was distraught, and Caralee and I felt that we just didn't know what to do about the situation. The church began to pray for Bledi. One morning at the children's meeting, I watched the little ones, some as young as five, praying their hearts out for Bledi. It hurt me to watch them crying out to the Lord with their eyes screwed tightly shut. I thought about how I might explain Bledi's death to them. Cancer could be a killer even in the West, but in Albania the medical treatment options were far harder to come by. I felt, though, that we must try to do something.

We decided to send out a fax to just about every Christian group we knew to ask them to pray with us for Bledi. Shortly, word came back from Pascack Bible Church in New Jersey that someone there had seen a TV programme about a hospital in the US which had had great success with cancer sufferers. It had seemed like such a ridiculous long shot, but they had

111

tracked it down by phoning around numerous TV stations, and contacted it.

The hospital was St Jude's in Memphis, Tennessee. We learnt that they had little available space and that the treatment costs there ran to hundreds of thousands of dollars. The only ray of hope was that they reserved a couple of places each year for children from underprivileged countries. They had suggested we submit them Bledi's details by fax.

I rode in the Land-Rover to Korçë to send the fax, and on the way home, as my eyes followed the ridgeline of the mountains to my left, a sudden feeling of peace came over me. I sensed the Lord telling me that he was going to take care of it – I distinctly sensed it. Three days later, as I left a meeting at the church, there was a commotion in the yard. A messenger had come down from Korçë with a fax from St Jude's. I fumbled to unfold the sheet of shiny paper and scanned it quickly. The hospital was saying that they were ready to admit Bledi and meet all of his medical costs!

Before I could even mention my joy to others, my head was spinning with all the logistical problems. The doctors were saying that Bledi had very little time left before his cancer would begin to spread into other organs. We needed to get him from Ersekë to Memphis in 72 hours. He needed a passport, a visa, legal papers and transportation to the airport in Tirana just to begin with. It was impossible. As I felt my stomach begin to twist with the stress, I remembered the words God had brought back to me in the beach house at San Diego: 'He will show you how to get everything done in the time that is given ...'

I set the wheels in motion immediately. Bledi's parents were told the incredible news. Back at our apartment, I asked Caralee if she would pack her bag so she could accompany Bledi as his translator. 'I've already done it,' she replied, holding my gaze. 'The Lord told me to this afternoon.' I was gobsmacked.

Shortly, Reshati knocked on our door, offering to help us get Bledi a passport. As we made our way to the police station together, Kujtimi, the state police chief, accelerated across the main square in his gold Mercedes. We needed his signature on a document for the passport and tried to wave him down, but his car raced on. I kicked the road stones in frustration. Twenty minutes later, however, as we waited at the station, he arrived back.

'What is it? What's happened?' he enquired curtly. Five kilometres down the road, he'd been overcome with a feeling of guilt at driving past us and ordered his driver to turn around. Reshati explained the situation. Kujtimi signed the papers, barked some orders at his men and then sped off again in his Mercedes.

When someone else managed to find the town notary, a gaunt man with bloodshot eyes, he was in an advanced state of drunkenness. We placed some documents before him, and he swayed around with the stamp in his hand trying to strike the correct spot. With a little assistance, he hit the mark and that was good enough.

We now had all the necessary paperwork, but we still needed to get Bledi to the American Embassy in Tirana by the following morning, a journey of at least five hours. At this point Mark Stoscher arrived back from a visit to Korçë. There he had spoken to the Mission Aviation Fellowship, and they had agreed to get a plane down to Korçë to fly Bledi to the capital first thing. It was all slotting into place. By noon the following day, Bledi and I were at the American Embassy, where the visa application was fast-tracked. I then toured the airline offices trying to book two tickets on a flight to the US. On my third visit to Swissair, they told me they had managed to clear two seats for us on their heavily booked flights.

Later in the day, Caralee and Bledi's father met us in Tirana, having driven there. By the early hours of the following morning,

Bledi and Caralee were on their way to New Jersey. From there they were relayed down to Memphis, and by the following night Bledi was under treatment.

As Bledi's father and I drove south back up the winding mountain road towards Lake Pogradec, the amazing sequence and speed of events began to sink in. The Lord had used so many people to achieve something that had seemed almost folly to hope for: the prayers of the children, the person who'd seen the TV programme in New Jersey, Reshati, Kujtimi, Mark and Caralee. In my mind now I had few fears for Bledi. If the Lord had pulled out all the stops to get him there, he would not fail when it came to following through. It also hit me, though, that Caralee was gone for the first time since we were married. I looked out at the patchwork of green fields way below and wondered when I would see her again.

Bledi's healing was not immediate. However, despite his ups and downs over the next six months, as he lost weight during chemotherapy and then regained it, the general trend was firmly towards recovery. The children at church sent him regular cards and recorded him songs, and others, including Mark, took over at Bledi's side in America. It was a full three months before Caralee returned home for a break from minding the boy. As a representative of all the believers who'd helped Bledi, and especially because she had flown with him to Memphis, Caralee was a hero in the eyes of the people of Ersekë. Reshati offered to organize meeting her in Tirana, and Kujtimi the police chief surrendered his gold Mercedes and driver to ferry her home.

As Reshati and I sped northwards in the car, with its smoked glass windows and special number plates denoting the chief's rank of lieutenant colonel, we enjoyed the instinctive salutes the vehicle brought us mile after mile along the roadside. We passed through the centre of Tirana, and as we drew closer to the airport district of Rinas we were waved to a halt by a police officer. Our driver slowed the Mercedes regally. Ahead of us was a procession of military vehicles and soldiers moving steadily across of our field of view with a stiff ceremonial pomp. There were regiments of Greek, Turkish and Albanian soldiers, each distinguishable by their flags. I watched the black two-headed eagle of Albania flap proudly past on its red background.

I figured there must be some sort of meeting of military chiefs happening at the airport. Our driver lowered the electronic window. The officer saluted him, and then spoke into his radio. A couple of minutes later, the officer's radio crackled with a message and he waved us forward. As we set off, the procession stopped and the soldiers and their vehicles edged awkwardly over to the side of the road to allow our car through. Reshati looked at me, his eyes widening as he smiled. 'Kapllani is showing his respect to Kujtimi,' he grinned knowingly. I felt like lowering myself into the leather seat. Colonel Kapllani, chief of police for the international airport and Rinas, had formerly been chief of police in his home town of Ersekë. He was now moving over the parading solders, with all the disrespect to their chiefs of staff, for his old comrade Colonel Kujtimi – only it was Reshati and me in the back! As the soldiers saluted us, we saluted back.

Colonel Kapllani had lined up his staff outside the terminal building to greet Kujtimi. Our driver drew the vehicle to a halt with professional smoothness and opened the rear passenger door. Reshati and I stepped out. For a moment, Kapllani looked at his staff and then back at us. A smile then split his face and he began to laugh.

'Reshati! What are you doing in Kujtimi's car?' he exclaimed. 'Do you realize I've just had three Balkan armies pull over for you?'

Reshati shuffled a little and began to explain what had happened with Bledi, and how we were actually on our way to collect Caralee at the airport. Kapllani was in fact delighted to learn about what the Lord had done for this young boy from his home town. He gestured for us to return to the car, and soon, as we followed Kapllani's black Mercedes, we were being waved through security checkpoints and barriers directly on to the runway of Tirana Airport. Shortly afterwards, the Swissair jet with its white cross on the tail fin came into view below the cloud base and touched down on the runway.

As it taxied to a standstill nearby, the driver drew us closer. Caralee was the first passenger down the steps, and her luggage was brought directly to the back of our Mercedes. She looked at me with curious surprise. 'What a welcome!' she smiled.

Reshati thanked Kapllani and the baggage handlers, and I overheard one of them ask: 'What's so special about this woman that she should be met on the tarmac of Tirana Airport?'

Reshati's reply made me smile: 'I think she is the Queen of Armenia.'

'Oh,' the other nodded, suitably impressed. Afterwards in Rinas, it was widely thought that she was.

To my mind, it was all a fitting reception.

This was 1996. Throughout 1995 and well into the current one, a number of 'investment firms' had set up their operations in Albania. The rates of return they were offering seemed to many in Ersekë and across the country like a prospect that was too good to refuse. Vefa, Gjalica, Xhaferi and Populli were the names of just some of the organizations making big promotional splashes and eliciting frenzied deposits from a people who had little or no experience of investment and feasible levels of return. Initially, with my background in economics, I knew that interest rates of 10 per cent a month were high but conceivable, but later the schemes began promising 30 per cent a month, which could only be sustained by drawing in more and more investors. I had read about similar 'pyramid schemes' establishing themselves in Russia and Romania before they collapsed disastrously, and the alarm bells were ringing loudly in my ears.

Across the country, people were selling their homes, their livestock and anything they could lay their hands on to invest in the schemes. For many, it was as if capitalism had finally arrived. This was how the West made money, it was felt, and after decades of Communism at last there was an opportunity to join the club. Over the summer of 1996, people were making plans and dreaming about how they would never have to work again.

It was deeply worrying to watch it spread through Ersekë like a sickness. In the cafés and bars there were two burning topics of conversation: the election results and investment firms. We warned those in our churches to steer clear of the schemes, and the believers responded well. The parents and families of those who attended, however, were often more difficult to convince. In Ersekë, I warned those who would listen that such rates could not be sustained for long, but more often than not the advice was met with dismissals.

I remember heated arguments with the father of one girl in the church's drama group. A proud man whose eyes would always slip away from my own, he would wave his hand sharply as if to brush aside my remarks. '*Kjo s'ka Kuptim!* No one in their right mind would take 12 per cent per annum from the Albanian Bank when you can get 30 per cent a month, Jani. You must think I'm crazy!' he shouted.

Such was the view of too many. Later in the year, he sat on the couch in our apartment, his shoulders bowed and his hand covering his eyes as he shook with grief. Along with his wife and three daughters, he was facing imminent eviction on to the dirt yard in front of their apartment block. He had staked everything that he could raise, and he had lost it all.

In the October of 1996, the bubble burst. The pyramid finance schemes began to collapse across Albania. Some people were more fortunate, noticeably those in authority, in recovering perhaps 50 per cent of all that they had invested. The majority of people were losing everything that they had staked: their homes, their livestock, their life savings. As the reality settled over Ersekë like a black weather front, the mood of the people turned to despair and hopelessness. The feeling among many was that capitalism as well as Communism had now failed them. As I made my way about the streets of the town on church business, I felt a rising sense of dread. When the new year began, the mood in Ersekë and across the rest of the country worsened. It began to turn to anger.

8 THE CROSS AND THE KALASHNIKOV

Late one afternoon in the first week of March 1997, a long convoy of trucks rumbled through Ersekë heading southwards. The people dotted around the central square watched uneasily as the young conscripts on board bounced past in their rough green canvas uniforms. The huge Chinese-manufactured trucks with their wide wheel arches shook the foundations of the apartment blocks. Political tension had been simmering across the country since the May elections of the previous year, but in recent months towns to the south of us – Vlorë, Sarandë and Gjirokaster – had spun into outright rebellion against the government. A state of emergency had been declared, and they were now sending troops down from the north in an attempt to bring the situation under control.

Recently, people had been protesting on the streets about their losses in the pyramid schemes and about the election results. In Ersekë square, as crowds had jostled and shouted angrily at the authorities, dogs had been set loose, sending people stumbling frantically out of their way. There was a fear in the air that something was about to happen.

Later that evening, the convoy thundered back through the town with the soldiers firing off their guns wildly as a frightened warning to anyone in their path. The story soon came through that they had arrived in the small town of Përmet, around 60 kilometres south of us, expecting to be welcomed as liberators. A skirmish had ensued, and the residents had risen up and attacked them. The convoy was fleeing along the road north to Korçë as if the whole of the south were against them.

Nachi, the young man in our youth group with round wire-framed glasses, telephoned us early the next morning with some troubling news about a missionary friend. Nachi was now stationed with the army in Leskovik, a small southern town that sat at the foot of a spectacular white rocky peak an hour's drive over the mountains.

'*Allo* Jani?' he shouted with a tense urgency. 'You've got to get down here. Joe is going crazy. Everyone is talking about how the Communists are coming up from Përmet to take Leskovik. He's saying he's going to swim the river for Greece – with his wife and son. The Greeks will shoot him if he tries. You've got to talk some sense into him!'

'Okay, Nachi. Give us a couple of hours,' I replied. I had known Joseph, the gentle giant from Florida, since the earliest of our days in Korçë, and I was worried for him – and about the news from Përmet. Quickly, along with a group of young men from the church, I set off for the town in a taxi. As we passed the white stone buildings of Ersekë's barracks, a large crowd was gathering and shouting at the guards. Later, as we entered Leskovik, we passed a police van in flames and sending up column of thick black smoke that drifted towards the rock peak high above the town. Four police officers sat forlornly watching their vehicle crackle and blacken. Everywhere in Leskovik, the men and youths had Kalashnikov rifles slung over their shoulders in readiness.

When we arrived at Joseph's house, he was pacing around and insisting that he had to leave Albania. A conflict was building up and he wanted out immediately. He was deeply troubled. We talked him out of fleeing over the mountains to

Greece, and later that day delivered him, along with his family, to Kapshtice border crossing. As I watched his frame grow smaller through the rear window, I considered the option of following him soon, but despite all events I felt at peace about remaining. Whatever happened now, I reasoned, we would take it one day at a time.

Crowds continued to gather on the streets in Ersekë throughout the following day. Outside the police station, the barracks and the arms depot at the far end of the pinewoods, the Socialists and others were demanding the right to arm themselves, shouting and threatening those who stood in their way. Later in the day, all three buildings were stormed and stripped of their stocks of pistols, rifles, grenades and ammunition boxes. Those who had taken them scattered back among the apartment blocks with their arms piled high, dropping them as they stumbled and ran.

The town police station was left ablaze from the raids. Along with Tero, Nachi and others, I helped with a relay of water buckets into the building until I was overcome with the smoke. My eyes were burning and my lungs felt tight as we made our way, an hour later, back across the main square towards our apartment.

Just off the main square, a young blond-haired man was holding a Kalashnikov up in the air and firing it off wildly. The echo cracked around the buildings, and I flinched at the sound. Across from him, a group of people were pinned flat to the dirt at the edge of an apartment block. As the weapon recoiled, the bullets were flying in all directions. It was clear that any minute somebody was going to get hurt. I knew the young man a little, and he was badly distressed.

'Ej ej ... get me more magazines for my gun, or I'll shoot someone!' he cried out angrily to those nearby. My heart was pounding with fear, but I felt I had to do something. I took off my jacket and held out my hands palm-upwards so that he could see I wasn't armed. I walked tentatively towards him. Soon we were close enough to talk, but he was lost in his mind, firing off the rifle into the sky. I could feel the hairs on the back of my neck standing on end and my hands were cold and sweating.

Behind me, a man arrived with a bag full of magazines. He tossed them forward and they clanked down on the road, close enough for me to pick up. I reached slowly down and took the bag's handles. '*Më jep ato!* Give me them,' he shouted, his voice almost breaking.

'You don't need them. It's okay,' I replied, trying to calm him down. 'You're going to hurt someone and you don't want that, do you?'

'Give me that bag,' he barked. He stepped towards me and reached out his arm to take it. As he did so, I grabbed him and hugged him firmly. At first he was taut, but then his body went limp as if it had slipped off his bones. The rifle clattered to the ground. He shook in my arms and then cried out in pain as he broke. '*Vëllezrit e mi.* My brothers,' I heard him say. 'My brothers are gone.'

The boys helped me put him into a car, and he was driven back to his village. I was still shaking an hour after he had left. I later learnt that three of his brothers had volunteered to help the Democrats put down an uprising in Vlorë, and they had not returned.

As soon as darkness descended on the town that evening, the noise of gunfire began. Away somewhere among the apartment blocks a short burst of rifle fire punctured the silence: 'tat-tat-tat-tat'. Moments later, from another quarter of the town the same noise cracked out in reply like some deathly mating call. Then it seemed that others joined in. The noise grew, as if there were a mass battle building up out on the streets. Rifles, pistols, semi-automatics and machine-guns were being fired, and grenades and tank bombs were exploding outside in a growing roar of sound that the walls of our apartment were too thin to mask. The window glass rattled with a ferocious wall of white noise like the hiss of a giant speaker-stack that went on hour after hour. In the briefest of let-ups, the silence was almost as intense, broken only by the braying of a traumatized mule.

Caralee and I lay together in the bedroom throughout the night, but sleep was impossible. I could feel her heart racing, and I was covered in a film of cold sweat. We held on to each other like interlocking clamps, and I fought with all my feelings to think clearly and logically about the situation. When the first light of the morning began to enter the room, I was exhausted. The noise at last began to die down.

There was a knock at our door shortly after dawn. Kujtimi, the chief of police, stood holding a pad of documents and looking uncomfortably apologetic. He explained that the police were pulling out of the town and would no longer be responsible for law and order.

'I can give you permission to arm yourselves legally, to guard your church building, if you want it,' he said with a hint at con-ciliation. I told him that we had not made such a decision. He left me a signed piece of paper, and I watched him hurry off down the apartment-block stairs.

I was determined to maintain some normality in my behav-iour and not be overcome by the situation, and a little later I left for a walk around the town. I stepped around the puddles in the muddy yard at the back of our apartment block and looked up at another long row of flats known locally as the Pallati Trenit ('train apartments'). Curtains were closed as if people were still deeply reluctant to face the new day. The air was damp and smelt heavy with gunpowder.

I walked over the spot where the young man had been firing his Kalashnikov the previous day. Ahead, the square was quiet;

there was no carnage. I realized now that though I had imagined a battle had been raging in the early hours, the reality was different. More likely was that as each person had fired off his stolen weaponry, others nearby had let off theirs as a warning that they too were now armed and ready to defend themselves. The real danger to the people of Ersekë was not coming up the road from the south, but breaking out on its own streets.

I had been thinking constantly about what Caralee and I should do, whether or not we should leave Albania because of such conditions. My mind kept dwelling on Jesus' words in the Gospel of John about the difference between the good shepherd and the hired hand. The hired hand leaves his flock when the wolf comes; the good shepherd remains. The words were important to me. I felt committed to staying and I knew that Caralee did, too – but I was afraid.

To help us with our communications in a town that still had wind-up phones to a single operator, I had acquired a portable ComSat satellite telephone on trial just two months earlier during a visit to the US. Now it was to prove invaluable. From the top of our apartment block, Mark and I lined up the little grey unit with the Indian Ocean Satellite, and I was able to make contact with friends in the US and the UK. Their voices were a tremendous comfort. I spoke regularly with a man named Mike Durante at Pascack in New Jersey, Korky Davey, the pukka yachtsman who headed up Open Air Campaigners in England's West Country, and others who listened and questioned us daily about our presence here. They challenged but they did not try to control, and I was grateful for that. Though many other foreign workers were leaving for their own safety, I felt the decision of whether to evacuate or not was ours. Mark and Ruth had similarly decided to remain and take it day by day, and their presence with us in the town was a great comfort.

Over the following week in Ersekë, the situation slid into a downward spiral. Throughout the nights the gunfire continued. To add to my concern, Caralee also told me that she was pregnant. I thought over appropriate names. If our child were a boy, I was of a mind to call him Lufta Civile ('civil war'); if twins, the second would be named Shkëmbim Zjarri ('exchange of fire'); and if a girl, Krisma ('gunfire sounds').

With the police now abstaining from any effective law enforcement and arms freely available to anyone from the abandoned barracks and arms depots (the army too had fled), anarchy broke loose like a vicious animal. At night, the criminal elements of the town took advantage of the situation and began looting the shops along the main street. In the mornings the glass would lie in shattered piles on the pavement, and the dropped spoils – tins, boxes and packages – would be crushed and strewn across the road.

What was perhaps most disturbing and disheartening was that, in the open daylight, we watched the ordinary residents join in the growing free-for-all. Close to our block was the town's kindergarten, a flat-roofed, two-storey building surrounded by a low breeze-block wall. From our apartment window, we saw our neighbours stumbling to and fro as they carried out its baby beds and play pens. Eventually, it was stripped of everything – heating system, doors, windows – as locusts would devour a cornfield. Even the tiles on the toilet floor were prised up and taken.

The bank was hit, the pharmacy and the school dormitory. The hospital even had its freezer for blood storage stolen. Just about any public building was becoming a target for opportunists. To me it all seemed like a myopic craziness; the people were robbing themselves.

On the first day that anarchy broke out in Ersekë, Tero had sprinted between apartment blocks checking up on many believers and delivering loaves of bread. He arrived at our door breathless and concerned for Caralee and me, and his courage and example touched us. In the circumstances, it now seemed crucial to keep tabs on all the believers. Almost everyone was staying at home with their doors firmly locked and barred to the mayhem out on the streets. We decided we needed to set up a monitoring system for everyone's care, and divided the church membership into cell groups, assigning a runner to regularly visit each person in their cell. Every morning, the runners began to meet at our apartment to report back on who was struggling – especially with fear, for everyone was afraid – and on whose food stocks were running low, and to act as a message switchboard. With Mark, Tero and others, I made my way among the *pallatet* with a nervous stealth while regularly someone nearby would empty the magazine of their Kalashnikov into the sky.

The visits strengthened everyone, and helped all the community of believers feel bound closer together. I also did what I could to help the Korçë and Bilisht churches set up similar systems: anarchy was sweeping through their towns, too.

As our system of runners re-established communication, we decided it would be good, for those who were ready, to meet together and pray for each other – and, crucially, for the town. Word soon came back through to us that more and more people wanted to attend, not just church members but their friends and families too. Such was the response that I felt the church building was going to be too small. In the circumstances, the central square seemed like the bold location. It was clear to me with an increasing urgency as the days were passing that the event needed to be felt beyond our community of believers. Casualties from the gunfire were mounting up each hour. Dozens had already lost their lives in Ersekë as bullets shot randomly into the air came down like hailstones and struck people as they fell. We made contact with Ersekë's Orthodox priest and the town's Moslem movement, and invited them all to stand with us in unity on the coming Sunday.

When the day came, I and others who had agreed to lead the public prayer meeting gathered on a concrete podium in the town square, facing the same cafés that had emptied for Caralee's sketchboard presentation during Project Resurrection. The early afternoon air was crisp and the ground was covered in patches of dirty, compacted snow; the crowd that gathered stood shuffling and rubbing their arms. The numbers grew rapidly until the square was almost full. Many people were venturing out of their homes warily for the first time in days. I had been praying and thinking about what I would say as my contribution to the gathering.

That morning, I had heard of an incident that underlined the tragic futility of the anarchy. 'Let me tell you about something that happened this morning in Pojan,' I began when it was my turn to speak. 'You all know how such things are happening here in Ersekë: but consider this. A bullet was fired into the air there, just like here, and it killed a young boy as it fell. Is that not enough of a tragedy? The boy's father then took his gun and shot the man who fired the gun. That man's brother took his gun and killed the boy's father. Do you know what happened then? The spiral of violence continued until thirty-one people now lie dead there!'

Even as I spoke, the 'tat-tat-tat' of rifle fire could be heard away over the apartment blocks.

'We are all responsible for our actions,' I appealed, looking down at the faces of those near the front. 'No one is enforcing the law here in Ersekë, but God's law still stands. One day, and that day might suddenly be upon any one of us in these times, we must all account for what we have done before God himself. Let us all take responsibility for what happens here in our town, and not claim that it is someone else's doing! We can choose now to come to God and he will show us the right way out of this. What will you choose for yourself, your family, and for Ersekë?'

Mark led the crowd in prayer, and I sensed a genuine level of contrition in the square. Many who were not known to me as believers stood with their heads lowered. As the meeting broke up and we left the square, people came forward to tell us that the town needed God's help, that they needed it, and that they would pray. In that moment, I sensed that the believers were shining. Despite our fear, we had a hope and confidence that was suddenly being thrown sharply into relief against those around us.

That evening, I heard of how one of the town's hooligans was speeding around in a black van he'd stolen from the funeral parlour, confiscating weapons from anyone he caught firing them. The meeting had made an impression.

With almost every public building in Ersekë falling under the sights of the looters, we had been getting ever more anxious about the church. We had taken out our computer school's PCs and mounted a 24-hour guard there, and so far the building had not been touched. We were now, however, hearing rumours that it was going to be hit, and the guards were reporting a white van full of men staking out the building late at night. We prayed for those who remained there to secure it through the night. Initially, when Kujtimi the police chief had left a document allowing us legal possession of arms, we had felt no need of them, but many in the church were now fiercely debating the rights and wrongs of the issue for hours. Was it ever permissible for Christians to bear arms? Was the disciple Peter not carrying a sword on the night of Jesus' arrest? Was it the weapon that was wrong *per se*, or the reason and the way that it was used? Should we lie down and surrender, and accept whatever those who were armed chose to do to us and our property? How much were we in danger of stepping over the line if we took up arms and then used them? How far did one defend oneself, or rely on the supernatural protection of the Lord? If our guards felt safer possessing them for deterrence purposes, should they be prevented from keeping them? Such were the difficult questions debated in Bible schools the world over, but for us they were no longer academic.

There was no unanimity of position among the believers on the issue, and it was left to each person to make their own decision before the Lord. The threats on the church building continued to intensify, though, with blasts of gunfire being shot over the roof to frighten the guards into fleeing. Some of the guards chose to carry weapons, and rounds were let off through the fruit trees into the night sky as a noisy deterrent to the thieves now biding their time beyond the rock walls.

Only days after the prayer meeting in the square, the situation in the town reached a further crisis point. There were now no food supplies left in the shops along the main street; in the anarchy no one was travelling to re-supply them. The bread factory had sold all its flour for fear of being robbed. There were no medicines left to treat the injured and dying in the hospital. Vast amounts of crystalline penicillin were needed to deal with the swelling ward of gunshot victims, and they just weren't storing enough for what had happened. Now more people were dying because of a lack of simple treatment, and to make matters worse the hospital had been looted again.

One evening we held a prayer meeting in the little side room of the church, and many of the teenage boys were present. Nachi stood up and addressed everyone. 'We keep talking about being light in darkness. Well, when are we going to be it?' he appealed.

One of the other boys added, 'Can't we get anything for the town from Greece? There must be some way we can do it!'

As it happened, I'd already spoken on the satellite phone to a doctor we knew at a Christian hospital in Thessaloniki. They had medicines there, but no one was willing to risk coming into Albania to deliver them. I told the boys about the conversation. At the end of the meeting, Nachi and Tero walked away in the darkness along the rubble road to the town centre. Half an hour later, they rumbled back to the church in a two-ton van that they'd managed to borrow. 'We'll drive to Greece if anyone will go with us,' they shouted through the window over the racket of the engine. From that moment, it was decided.

In the early morning light of the following day, we formed a convoy of a couple of two-ton trucks and two taxis to drive to Kapshtice border crossing. I felt very apprehensive about driving through open country, but determined to make the journey. Inside each vehicle we had a couple of Kalashnikov rifles. It was felt that at times en route it could be necessary to show that we were fully capable of defending ourselves if we were threatened: the roads were now rife with banditry and hijackings. On a number of occasions, we were to drape them outside the trucks' cabin doors as a visual deterrent.

About an hour after we had left Ersekë, we entered the small shambling village of Placa. Ahead of us on the road, the residents had dragged some artillery guns from a nearby army depot and interwoven them to form a barricade. We slowed our vehicles to a gradual standstill. A group of the villagers drew their weapons and waited cautiously ahead of us, some twenty yards behind their defences. I glanced across at Mondi, my driver, and he returned a look of caution. Together with a youth nicknamed Greedy Lili, we stepped down from the truck and walked steadily over to talk to them.

'*Tungjatjeta*,' I shouted. 'We are from Ersekë. We are driving to Kapshtice for medicines.' The men eyed us for a minute.

Then they nodded and began rolling the guns to the roadside to clear a space through the centre.

'You are crazy!' they shouted as we passed through. 'Go safely. *Mirupafshim.*'

The villagers' barricade was a simple act of self-preservation. They wanted to ensure that no one passing through was going to assault them or loot their homes.

Around three hours later, we drove into a further situation in Korçë. To our amazement, we watched a group of teenagers launching an attack on the town's lemonade factory. Inside it, another group of young men were attempting to defend it. The raid flared up suddenly around our convoy. There was little we could do but pull over, keep our heads down low, and peer over the dashboard as events developed. The attackers' first attempts to take the building were repelled by an anti-aircraft gun mounted on the roof. They retreated, only to return twenty-five minutes later with a tank. As they pounded the factory walls, the brick fragments tumbled back into the road.

Though we had come through enough, I felt even more anxious about the final five kilometres of the route to the border crossing. Here, the narrow pot-holed road snaked upwards along the course of a stream, shouldered steeply on either side by overlooking hills. It was the perfect setting for an ambush; blackened car wrecks dotted the roadside as forbidding reminders.

At about 1.30 p.m., a couple of kilometres past the town of Bilisht, we drove into yet another conflict situation. Two armed gangs were attacking each other, and one of them, assuming that we were part of their rival's manoeuvres, suddenly opened machine-gun fire on us. Rounds of ammunition raked the ground around our wheels, sending up thin lines of dust. I gripped the door handle, praying for our lives, and not one bullet hit the vehicle. God was surely protecting us.

Moments later, I noticed a military helicopter coming out of the distance. It began to dip down towards us. As it drew closer, the gust from the rotor blades whipped up the dust in swirling clouds, and it assumed a position about fifty feet above us, hovering like some mechanical guardian angel. I was utterly stunned. The Greek army must have had their contacts in the hills watching the road below! They had sent in a special forces unit specifically to escort us up the pass to Kapshtice, and its arrival scattered our attackers. I struggled to grasp what had made them come in to help us. I'd never really had a great deal of respect for Greek soldiers, but here they were in Albanian airspace risking their lives for our small mercy run.

Half an hour later, at the border crossing, the Albanian post had been abandoned. The building was charred and smoking and the barrier pole lay at an angle on the roadside. Two hundred yards further along, the Greek guards tumbled out of their building and stood shaking their heads as we drew up. As we emerged from the vehicles, my old friend the customs colonel set out a table and chairs, poured us some glasses of ouzo and began slapping my back.

'Crazy! Crazy!' said another officer placing a finger on his temple and twisting it. I was shaking but high on exhilaration. Barth Campanjen, the roly-poly Dutchman, and others who had helped transport food and medicines in a five-ton truck from Thessaloniki, were also waiting. They walked across to meet us, and we held each other firmly.

The trucks were loaded swiftly by all hands present with salt, flour, oil, rice, and enough crystalline penicillin for the hospital back in Ersekë and for those in Korçë and Leskovik too. Our friends in Greece were worried for our safety and did not want us to leave. I felt concerned about our journey home, but I felt wrapped anew in a strengthened confidence of the Lord's presence with us. It was a moment of the highest sensation of his power and preserving favour. Everyone in the convoy felt that way.

We honked the horn as a further goodbye to our friends as we left Kapshtice half an hour later. The journey home was in normal circumstances a two-hour run. It took us a further five hours, however, stopping and driving around further situations on the road through Korçë, and back southwards into the country.

That evening I was deeply relieved to arrive back in Ersekë. After about half an hour, though, I could feel my arms and legs trembling as the realities of the day sank in. A terrible shock was also awaiting us. Until that moment, no one in the church had been injured in all the mayhem. Now, we learnt that a young boy, Altin, had been caught in the cross-fire of some dispute and had taken a bullet in the liver while we had been at the border. Thankfully, over the next few days the medicines we'd brought in helped him pull through, though he lost a large piece of the organ from the injury. Later that evening, the father of one of the boys in the church was killed, shot by his own Kalashnikov in a tragic drinking incident, the precise circumstances of which were misty. We had begun to think that we were untouchable, and I fell from an incredible high into a deep trough.

That evening we made the decision to return the following morning on a further run for aid supplies. With the help of churches and many individuals in Greece, the UK and the US, we kept up our aid runs, driving almost every other day for the next six weeks. We continued to bring in deliveries of medicine, flour and salt so the bakers could make bread, and other consignments for the town. I devised an arrangement to sell the foodstuffs at wholesale price to the shops and pass on the proceeds to the town council so they could pay those living on government benefits. In the anarchy these had simply ceased.

With the help of our runners, who kept their eye on the needs of everyone in their cell-groups, we passed out food packages to the believers.

The route to Kapshtice was always a dangerous one. Robberies were widespread on the roads, and regularly we had to divert around skirmishes in the villages. On the fourth run we made, we narrowly avoided an ambush. As we approached the summit of Qafë e Qarrit through the pine trees and oak shrubs, we noticed a group of bandits waiting ahead of us at a hairpin turn. We heard the crack-crack of gunshots into the air as a command to us to brake. We began to accelerate towards them. As we drew closer, a hand grenade was tossed in front of the truck. The driver swung the wheel sharply as we cornered. The grenade went off with a terrific 'wumpf'. We accelerated on, and I blew out a huge breath of air. I watched the men group around the scorched tarmac as they grew smaller in the truck's wing mirror. It had damaged the road, but by God's grace it hadn't damaged us.

As the weeks of March and April went by, many people in Ersekë let us know their appreciation for the deliveries we were bringing in, but one group of men decided they would try to work the situation to their advantage. One evening, Caralee discovered a folded piece of lined paper pushed under our apartment door. The anonymous note was demanding that $10,000 be placed at a point drawn on a map of the town's football pitch. It was signed with a death threat and instructions that it be done in 48 hours' time. Caralee and I were troubled by it, but as the hours passed I tried to figure out who had left it.

In the early hours of the morning before the deadline, members of the blackmailing group fired their machine-guns below our bedroom window to emphasize their point. The noise woke us with a violent start, but it brought out others in our block who chased them off with counter-blasts of rifle fire. As the group fled, through the window I glimpsed the heavy-set form of a man as he strode quickly away. It was difficult for either of us to sleep again that night, but I had figured out who was behind it.

The next day I decided to ignore the deadline, but sent word to the group that I would meet them in a café in the town square. I had not told anyone else in the church about the meeting, for fear of placing them at risk, so when Tero suddenly arrived to accompany me I was deeply glad of his support. We made our way across the central square to a large café on the corner opposite the town museum. Though Ersekë was busy, there were no other customers inside except a group of a dozen men waiting around two wooden tables drawn together. It seemed the café had been cleared for our arrival. Tero and I walked uncomfortably towards them and took two chairs. The men all watched us, some hidden behind sunglasses, others trying to gain a little psychological advantage.

'We've heard you speaking disrespectfully about Albanians,' a man with thick, brown curly hair began. 'And you, Tero ... Why are you siding with this foreigner? You are an Albanian, aren't you?'

'I am,' retorted Tero, 'but some things go deeper than being Albanian. We are both believers, and he is my brother.' I was moved by his reply.

The man turned back to look at me. 'So, Jani, you've brought our payment,' he said.

'I have no payment for you,' I replied, trying to appear unafraid.

The man leant forward, with his elbows on the table. 'You're a foreigner here, just a lonely Englishman thousands of miles from your home,' he shouted. 'There is no government. There are no police in this town. We're in charge here now and we can do what we want with you. What is to stop us killing you now? Why don't you think about that?'

'When I die, I know where I'm going, and I'm not afraid of that. Do you know?' I shouted back angrily. 'So if you are going to do it, why don't you do it here and now?' I edged my chair back from the table. 'You are just a bunch of adolescents throwing your weight around because you've picked up a crate of Kalashnikovs. We've heard enough of your threats.'

'You think that you are big, eh?' the man spat, his face reddening with aggression. 'Well, who's going to protect you?'

'Our God is bigger than all of you,' Tero put in. 'Think about that!'

I pushed back my chair further and stood up to leave. One of the group grabbed hold of my arm. I pulled it away. Tero and I began to walk quickly towards the door. Two of the men followed us, shouting after us as we stepped into the road, 'Where do you think you are going? Get back here!'

The confrontation was now out in the square and within the ears of many. 'So you are making death threats?' I shouted, glancing at passers-by. 'Then if you are going to kill us, go ahead and do it! We've finished talking to you.'

We turned and faced them. The two men now realized that their private scheme was public. They looked around them hesitating, and then retreated furiously back inside the café. My heart was pounding and I felt a little sick as Tero and I walked back towards our apartment block, but we were not to have any more trouble from the gang from then on. Word got around the town about what they were trying, and it was very unpopular.

The aid deliveries brought a level of organization to the town, and many believers were complimented by friends, family and those in their apartment blocks for the way that they had brought others hope and new confidence. I felt truly proud of them. Our church community was held high in the esteem of many. Mark and I, together with many others, did what we could to be catalysts for peace. We kept up the habit of walking the streets of Ersekë early in the mornings, talking to those we met loitering or brandishing their weapons. It was still difficult to sleep for longer than a couple of hours a night at a stretch; the noise of guns and grenades was rattling and pounding on incessantly. Regularly in the conversations we struck up, we would try to question people about where they thought their actions were taking their country, and remind them of their own mortality with the latest tragic stories that were unfolding every day.

I remember one group of young men I spoke to many times, who had stolen a high-wheeled van from the local electricity company and armed themselves.

'Nuk e di! We don't know where it is all going. It would be better if someone brought the situation under control,' one of the boys confided to me.

I felt both guilt and regret for never challenging them directly to turn their hearts to the Lord. In the early hours of one morning, they met their demise in an incident with another gang at the town's chicken restaurant. Someone had pulled a gun, another had shot back, and like a scene in a Wild West bar the ensuing gunfight left the entire gang, the restaurant owner and the waiter dead in a pool of blood. Such events were commonplace in the country.

In a further tragic incident, two young men from Ersekë were practising shooting pistols in the pinewoods west of our apartment block. One of them, assuming he had fired all six bullets in the barrel, pointed it at his cousin's head for a joke and squeezed the trigger. He had only fired five. Mark spent time with the family helping them to come to terms with their loss, as far as anyone could, and I was proud of the way he comforted them. Accidents with guns, bullets and explosives were happening frequently.

A particular practice also spread fear among all families with daughters. Holger told me of a not untypical incident which happened in his wife's family's apartment block in Korçë. Three men, clutching Kalashnikovs and with their faces concealed in black balaclavas, knocked on the door of a family there. They demanded that the daughter of the house be handed over. The father and brother resisted, exchanging fire with the men and killing them in the stairwell. When they pulled off the masks they discovered the men were their upstairs neighbours. Neighbour was setting on neighbour in the anarchy.

It was so hard to comprehend the craziness and futility of what was happening. Over a three-month period, I attended around sixty funerals. Often I would be asked to share a word, and I would return again and again to the theme of the vanity of human actions, the 'chasing of the wind' with life, or I would point to the fact that each person was responsible before God and could play their part in changing the situation for the better. Many times I thought of the days recorded in the Old Testament's book of Judges, where anarchy and lawlessness were rife among the people of Israel. Each person was doing what they saw fit in their own eyes in present-day Albania, and man's inhumanity to man was an appalling thing to behold. I thought also of the Arabic proverb that says, 'It is better to have two hundred years of tyranny than one day of anarchy', and witnessing the effects of total lawlessness I found myself in some sympathy with it.

Albania and Ersekë began to calm down to a degree as the fruit trees in the churchyard grew full once more with blossom. The army and the police did not finally enforce law and order, they had been too afraid of personal reprisals, but the people themselves grew sick of the chaos and allowed them to take back control. Many of the worst political hooligans and criminal opportunists had wiped each other out with their weaponry, and a kind of understanding settled over Ersekë. The people termed it *Mirë kuptim*, 'good understanding', a euphemism for what essentially meant: 'Don't touch me, and I won't touch you. Don't interfere with my business, and I won't interfere with yours.' Everyone was still armed and more than capable of retaliation. The Socialists had manipulated the people's anger over the pyramid schemes, the Democrats had manipulated the fear of the return of Communism, and the chaos that had ensued was beyond any of their calculations. Most of the public buildings in Ersekë had been ransacked, including the high school we had renovated, but our church remained untouched. Tero and others had risked their lives in defence of more than its bricks and mortar.

Two and a half months after it had all begun with the convoy of trucks thundering through our town on their way to Përmet, a couple of lonely armoured personnel carriers rolled into Ersekë with Italian soldiers on board, peering around uncertainly in their black-feathered hats. The international community had arrived to organize the peace.

9 FRUIT TREES IN THE CHURCHYARD

Life in Ersekë began to drift back to a degree of normality. The shops started trading again along the high street, selling their imported foodstuffs from Greece, Italy and Turkey, and the fruit and vegetable market was busy again with people stocking up on locally grown watermelons and peppers. The electricity, which had been off for long periods of the anarchy as no one had dared man the stations, returned for the majority of the day. With the help of the international community, a coalition government was formed over the summer, and elections were then held that returned the Socialists to power. It was on a warm August Sunday, a couple of months after the peacekeeping force had arrived, that I had a sense of emerging from the darkest of times since our arrival in Albania. Believers from the churches in Korçë, Bilisht and Libonik felt safe enough to travel down over Qafë e Qarrit to our church in Ersekë, and we felt safe enough to hold a large gathering for the first time in six months.

We had been in the habit of baptizing new believers in the cold, clear waters of Lake Pogradec each summer, but the town of Pogradec and many other places in the country were still not the safest of areas. Huge stocks of rifles, pistols and grenades remained at large among the population and little of it had been returned. Banditry and armed skirmishes were still flaring up in pockets, and some roads were best avoided. So for the first time ever, we baptized our new believers, forty-six of them, in a large metal bathtub at the rear of our church. The volleyball court and the lush grass around the fruit trees were packed with people of all ages, shaking hands and embracing.

As many people met again for the first time since the winter, we shared stories and incidents of the things that we had witnessed and passed safely through. There were accounts of real courage and selflessness. Angela, Bledi and Tero had scurried over a hundred children to their homes from a meeting at the church as the rifle fire cracked around them on the first day the anarchy broke out in Ersekë. Holger's wife, Zhenka, had walked alone up the open highway from Korçë to Maliq just to see what she could do for the believers there. Many had taken tremendous personal risks to visit and encourage other believers, and I felt proud of them. We had all been challenged to go deeper in our walk with the Lord. As everything around us had been breaking apart, our dependency on him to hold our lives together had been tested to the limit.

We worshipped noisily together, with three groups of musicians leading an enthusiastic chorus of praise. Each time another person was lifted up out of the cool water in the tub, looking slightly stunned by their immersion, it seemed like an offering of thanksgiving to God with another life of service. Each church paid tribute to the other with heartfelt applause. By God's grace we had overcome and been able to shine by example in ways that had made a deep impression in the lives of many around us. As I watched the meeting break up and people drifted through the church gates, under the vines now swelling with ripening bunches of green grapes, it felt as if the night had passed and a new day had begun.

Only a week before the baptismal service, though, Caralee and I had a number of deeply anxious days about her pregnancy.

Caralee had been experiencing both bleeding and cramps, and we grew concerned that remaining in Albania throughout all the stress of the anarchy might have affected her and our child. Some of our friends and contacts had raised such concerns themselves, and I felt under terrific pressure about the decision we had made to stay in Ersekë. When we had been trying for a child in the February, how could we have known that anarchy would sweep through our town in less than a month?

At the end of August, Caralee flew to England a couple of weeks before our child was due, and I followed shortly after. The problem was never clearly diagnosed, but we learnt that it wasn't a serious threat to her pregnancy. We rested and relaxed in the West Country at the garden bungalow of Korky Davey of Open Air Campaigners, and on 9 September, after a long labour, our baby girl was born at Bristol's Southmead Hospital. She was eight pounds in weight with dark curly hair and blue eyes. It was a wonderful moment. Despite all the names that had passed through my mind back in March as the mortar bombs had echoed around the apartment blocks – Krisma ('exchange of fire') being my favourite – we settled on the name Ashlie, from the Hebrew word *asher* meaning 'happiness', for that is what she brought us.

Back in Ersekë, as the first months of Ashlie's life passed, I would ask myself, 'Will she be insecure because of all the tensions of the time when she was growing in the womb?' How could I tell? But it soon became clear that she was in fact a deeply happy and secure little baby. Sometimes I would sneak up on her quietly in play and roar like a lion, but whatever I did it didn't seem to scare her one jot. I do believe that God preserved and protected Ashlie from any ill consequences, for I felt sure that it was right for us to remain in Albania through all its tribulations.

The year of 1998 began with our first ever wedding in the Ersekë church. Angela, the girl with the sad eyes who had taken a copy of the Gospel of John from me at the football stadium outreach in Korçë and had since become one of our most dedicated children's workers, had been engaged to Bledi for over a year. Bledi, the one-time wisecracking hooligan in a leather jacket whom I had had to evict from our meetings during Project Resurrection, had matured into a children's worker himself, and was a key musician in our worship band.

Angela had experienced many difficulties with her family since conversion but had stood firm in her faith despite them, whilst carrying many burdens. Being eleven years older than her fiancé put further stresses upon her and Bledi. For the wedding day, however, the families came together to give their blessings, which was a miracle in itself. The church was packed out once more for a wonderful day of celebration, and as a recognized pastoral authority I was able to read them their vows, and then wait with real expectation for their lives to grow together in God.

With the ransacking of almost all public buildings in Ersekë during the chaos, there was now a tremendous need for reconstruction. Officials in the town asked the church if we could help at all, and this was something that we had wanted to do. In the early days of the anarchy, we had watched with sadness as the town's kindergarten was stripped of everything within its walls, knowing that the real losers would be the youngest of the young. There was now no facility at all for them to be nurtured in preparation for school. It was this building that we had a heart to see renovated. Two Christian businessmen with charitable foundations in the US graciously made funds available to us; they had been touched by the witness of the believers, and wanted to show them their support for the things that they had passed through. Tero was appointed project manager and he began to do an excellent job of overseeing a team of twenty builders from the town. They took their orders and directions from him, and he, still only 22 years old, kept on top of what was, I knew full well, a difficult task. He began the process of rebuilding the smashed surrounding wall, re-laying the prised-up floor tiles, fitting new windows and doors, replumbing and rewiring; and workers from the town were not ungrateful for some solid employment.

As long as we had been in Ersekë, employment prospects in the town had never been very good. Following the crisis, however, and the destruction of both business property and infrastructure, unemployment was running at 70 per cent.

Outside the state sector and café or store ownership, the only other employment involved gathering leaves and flowers on the slopes of Mount Gramoz, to be sold, often for medicinal use, in Italy – a hard day's labour, and seasonal at that. There was a desperate need for jobs. It had been on my heart to try to do something to help ease the situation, and now, with the beginning of a new year, it seemed like a good time to develop some projects. As well as evangelism and church planting, I felt that such initiatives were integral to a full and holistic sharing of the gospel.

As a lover of the British chip, I had noticed that the local potato was a somewhat shrivelled and puny vegetable. The seed stock around Ersekë had degenerated over many years of use without replacement. So I set to work with Reshati. We earmarked 15 acres of his family's land in the mountains to the north, and imported some high-quality Dutch potato seed. Through the year, we brought on a new crop of potatoes at three times the local yield per acre – and they were good for chips! The project employed seven people, and we sold our harvest at an eventual profit of $700. We hoped that it might stimulate better potato production in the region, but to do it ourselves was proving too much of a time-consuming business. We were happy eventually to step back as a church and hand on the baton to a Dutch Christian development agency when they moved into the area.

Caralee also took the lead in developing a project to produce hand-knitted Jaeger wool sweaters for sale through contacts in England, Holland and America. She and Bledi's mother, Xhani, worked long and hard for many hours to make a success of the scheme. The sweaters themselves were fabulous. They were produced by the town's women in their homes after they'd received initial training and supervision. At its peak, the enterprise provided a good income for thirty families in the town, but Caralee and Xhani always had a battle to keep up the quality of the work. Selling the items in the quantities necessary in the West was never an easy process, either. We felt as the months passed that this and the idea for the potato plantation had come more from own hearts than from the Lord, yet he nevertheless honoured what we had tried to do and preserved the projects as they ran their courses.

When we had first entered the country in 1991, the Old Testament had yet to be translated into the Albanian language, and it was a further two years before full copies of the Bible were available for use in the embryonic churches. As for other Christian books, we knew of very few titles published at all in the first three years of our work there. My good friend Barth Campanjen, the roly-poly Dutchman, had immediately seen the need for books as an important means of helping the growth of the country's new believers, and I had caught hold of the same idea. Reading would be essential for self-discipleship in the growing churches. We had kept the idea in prayer and four years earlier, with Holger translating and Mark arranging printing in the US, we had published our first translation,

I Married You by Walter Trobisch, a biblical introduction to marriage. This had in hindsight been the seed of an enterprise that had steadily grown, as we had worked with translators, editors and designers to produce Albanian language versions of, among others, *The Cross and the Switchblade* by David Wilkerson and *Basic Christianity* by John Stott. We had now reached the stage where we felt ready to establish a permanent publishing operation to serve the whole evangelical community of the country.

Throughout the late spring, builders piled up bricks and sand in the middle of the road and added a further floor to the top of an out-building in the corner of the churchyard. There we established the office of Shigjeta (Arrow) Publishing. A young man called Doni, one of the original group of 'disciples' chosen by Mark during Project Resurrection, had continuously grasped the vision for the work and was to become our Director. Our aim was to try to publish a new Christian title every month, and as the venture progressed during the year we published Albanian language versions of *I Dared to Call Him Father* by Bilquis Sheikh, *The Master Plan for Evangelism* by Robert Coleman and *Can Man Live Without God?* by Ravi Zacharias.

I felt excited that we had crossed over the line from developing a hobby to running a professional operation. It had taken us four years of practice before we'd reached the stage where we felt ready to take the step, and the same amount of time for the early converts to mature enough to take such tasks on board for themselves. Sometimes it seems that the Lord gives a vision and it comes to fruition driven with a sovereign speed; it had been that way as the football stadium outreach had built up momentum over 48 hours in Korçë. At other times such visions require much prayer, planning and organization, and that was how it was with Shigjeta Publishing.

Early that spring, a sovereign work began to unfold that was to us both amazing and unexpected. A letter arrived out of the blue from a man who introduced himself as Malcolm Greenwood. In his formally written, neatly typed letter, he explained how, ten years earlier, he had travelled into Albania on a tour tightly controlled by the Communist authorities, praying covertly for the people as he went. During the tour, the bus had made an unscheduled stop in Ersekë for an hour. Here he had taken some photos of a group of young children and been praying for them ever since. He continued to explain that he'd heard about the work the believers were doing here now – and then came his surprising suggestion. He said that he would like to be involved in an orphanage, and wondered how the church would feel about having one.

It seemed all very sudden to us, and we felt a little reserved in our response to his idea: we'd had people making way-out suggestions to us before. We wrote back to say that we would like him to explain a little more about what he had in mind, and – out of politeness – that we would be interested to see his photos.

Malcolm's photos arrived in a second letter at the end of April, and when we looked at the group of around half a dozen boys we began to sit up. Three of them were among the group of young men who had stepped forward for Christ during Project Resurrection, Bledi, now married to Angela, included! It was a moment of profound realization. We had thought that their changed lives were a product of our ministry, but they were a deeper part of God's plan. He weaves his own purposes through time, and we just play our part in that.

As we discussed Malcolm's idea with the church and passed around the photos, we kept the matter in prayer. We began to realize how close to many people's hearts the issue of orphans had been, and a positive feeling towards the idea grew among us. Angela remembered the pain and anguish of our involvement with the orphanage in Korçë, and our prayers and desire to see a well-run sanctuary for the children. Tero was in tears as he remembered how the teams from Korçë and the US had taken little Koli, with his goatskin vest, under their wing. It had made a deep impression on him at the time. I couldn't help but reflect that if Vito had been under proper care, she would never have run the dangers of the organ trade in Vlorë.

Malcolm, an unassuming translator from the English Midlands, came to visit us in Ersekë at the beginning of May. He met the young men he had been praying for for many years, and a group of us told him about our experiences with orphans in Albania. Together we talked things over. The idea was raised that it would be wonderful to see a family-like home that would take care of a group of children until they were ready to stand on their own two feet. Malcolm liked the idea, and we prayed together about it.

Two months after he left us, he sent us an e-mail. In it he explained that an uncle of his had died, and that he had inherited a considerable sum of money. He now felt that the Lord was calling him to give the money to set up an endowment for the establishment of an orphanage run by our church in Ersekë.

Although we had talked about it and all been of a mind that such a place was desperately needed, none of us had really had the faith to believe that God would provide the money for it in one big slam of the table, but that is what he did. The leadership of the church decided to press ahead. A suitable old property was available for purchase directly across from the church building. We bought it and Tero began the process of supervising its rebuilding and conversion.

Caralee and I had never imagined being involved in such a venture. We did not think that we had the time for it, but we knew that God had already planned the people to work there, because he had brought so many other things together. Through Malcolm's appearance, I was reminded once more how God works through a wide body of people, and how he builds and builds on what he is planning. The moment impressed upon me again that, instead of doing what we choose and then asking the Lord to bless it, service is so much a matter of keeping in step with the Lord: sensing what he is preparing and following that. Jesus summed it up: 'I see what the father is doing, and I do the same.'

The year had seen the development and fruition of many projects, and now my role as a pastor was changing, too. As the leaders of the churches we had planted had emerged and matured – Holger in Libonik, Arjan in Bilisht, Aliu in Vashmi, Niko, Tero, Elisi and Doni in Ersekë, and many others in the children's and teenagers' ministries – they had taken on the daily duties of preaching and pastoring those in their care. I in turn had become a pastor to the pastors, and my focus had changed from evangelist–preacher to elder. It was a deeply satisfying phase to have reached, not for myself but for the church. After six years of maturing, the Albanian leadership was truly stepping up to bat. A movement of believers in the southeast of the country was beginning to run on its own, independent of us and other foreign missionaries.

In the beginning, it had been necessary to walk every day alongside those who were growing into the roles, then less frequently as they developed. I had tried not to pass the ball over until they were ready, nor to keep a hold of it because I still liked the feel. Over the summer, they had run street-preaching campaigns around the country themselves, as well as other projects leading unbelievers. They had taken them in their stride to such a degree that I felt they were no longer being challenged to grow.

As 1998 drew to a close, my thoughts began to turn towards a programme to take the leadership further. Over the years since we had come here, they had all, by and large, had the same church experiences and been exposed to the same small pool of literature and visiting foreign speakers we had managed to bring over. I figured that if a group could be taken abroad to meet a number of key Christian leaders in both First and Third World settings, then the whole Albanian church would benefit, and they could share their experiences with the next generation of believers. So this was my plan. I began to sketch out a programme to take them to the hugely successful Willow Creek Church in Chicago and to the expanding Christ Apostolic churches of Nigeria, to meet Christian business leaders in New York, and also to visit the Holy Land.

In the early months of 1999, I continued with the preparations for the programme, but all of our eyes were being continually drawn to the north of the country as we watched the TV news broadcasts. Ethnic Albanians from the Serbian-run region of Kosova were fleeing along the road from Prizren to the border, crossing north of the Albanian lakeside town of Kukes. Behind them, columns of smoke were rising above their villages. The stories they were bringing with them of evictions and executions were deeply disturbing but without independent verification. The refugees' faces, though, were wrought with trauma. At our services we began to pray about the situation. We were over 13 hours away from Kukes, along poorly surfaced roads, close to the southernmost tip of the country and in just about the worst position to help them. I had been sketching out my leadership challenge, but what was threatening to embroil Albania was looking like prospect enough.

10 SUNRISE OVER KOSOVA

When Beni Zylyftari, the current state chief of police, sent his chauffeur to wake me up in the early hours of the morning during the first week of April, the honking of his Mercedes horn sounded like an alarm in my head. As I peered down from our apartment block into the lane below, the headlights glared in the darkness. Moments later, there was a hammering on the door, and Beni's chauffeur stood there, breathing heavily.

'Quickly, quickly!' he shouted. 'They are coming, Jani, they are coming! The refugees will be here in a couple of hours!'

As I made my way through the town, picking my way around the dark, icy puddles, the questions I'd been building up for weeks began to turn over in my mind. It had been agreed that we at the church would act as a staging post for the town. But how much responsibility might fall on our shoulders after that? What condition would they be in? How many would come? And how would we cope? As the church had prayed for the Kosovars, many of us had felt strongly touched by the spirit of Matthew 25: 'Whatever you do for one of the least of these brothers of mine, you do for me.' I now felt a strengthening determination to serve. Up ahead of me the lights of the church were already on, and soon we were beginning to make what preparations were possible. We positioned a couple of tables as a reception desk to take down names and piled up the few blankets we had in readiness; downstairs in the kitchen, the water heater was in action ready for tea and hot soup. After around an hour there was little more that we could do.

A single coach drew into the centre of Ersekë at around 4 a.m. The night air was cold and the stars were bright in the cloudless black sky. I remember the faces of those on board pressed to the windows, anxiously surveying the strange town awaiting them. They watched cautiously as Beni and I approached the door of the coach and climbed up its steps.

Beni introduced himself. 'You have come to the town of Ersekë. You will be cared for here,' he announced.

'Where are we?' shouted one man angrily. 'Where the hell is Ersekë?'

'Are we in Greece?' snapped another man. There were gasps of fear and a woman began to sob.

'You are in Albania,' continued Beni. 'There is no reason to be alarmed.'

'We're staying here,' the man shouted back.

Beni and I walked along the coach aisle, trying to reassure them that it was safe to get off. After five minutes, one old man in a white fez stepped down from the coach. I showed him around the rooms where he and the others would be spending the night, and he returned to talk to his family. They now came down from the coach into the street. Others began to follow cautiously.

As Mark, Angela and others directed them into the building, a woman suddenly stumbled towards me in the darkness, weeping and bubbling over with words. 'Do you remember me? I believe in the God of Gani,' she cried. 'I believe in the God of Gani!'

As I tried to calm her down, I recognized her face. She was the mother of Gani, a man I'd met in Kosova who was now leading a church in Tirana. Gani had been regarded by his

Muslim family as a renegade. His mother told me that when she had crossed the border near Kukes, it had been Christians – 'Gani's people', she called them – who had given her water. Now she had arrived in Ersekë, and believers had met her here. It all made a deep impression. The following day, we organized her journey to her son in Tirana.

The group of around fifty Kosovars was encouraged inside the church building, and then their condition became more apparent. The smell of their clothing, casual and intended for wearing inside their houses, had an unsettling odour of fear about it. They had not changed since, three weeks earlier, they'd fled their homes with no forewarning and made for the mountains or the road to the border with Albania. One woman shuffled past me in her ruined slippers.

The refugees' faces were harrowed and lined, their skin pasty and their hair thick with sweat. Many were silent and withdrawn and obviously in a deep state of shock. All of them glanced ever cautiously around. We took down names and gave out hot drinks and all the blankets we had. Soon they began to collapse into exhausted sleep, until the floors of all three rooms in our church were covered. For many, it was the first night with a solid roof over their heads since they had left their towns and villages.

By the time I picked my way along the pot-holed road to our apartment, the puddles were reflecting the dawn sky.

Later that morning a further coach-load arrived. After the 14-hour journey down from Kukes following their flight into Albania, these Kosovars too were exhausted, in shock and confused about where they had been sent. We received them at the church and showed them into the old kindergarten building next door. They had nothing with them but the clothes on their backs, and we had only the stone floors of empty rooms for them to lie down on. Outside there was still snow on the ground. I tried a little humour to lighten a few faces, but they would simply break down in tears. I could read the expressions of those I led to the rooms: many were professional people used to a comfortable lifestyle in Kosova, and to be evicted to our town and to this was a further psychological kick. I felt that I really did not know what to do for them, except to try to improve their conditions as we went along.

We quickly gathered what money we had in the church funds, together with the $700 profit from the potato project, and I began frantically organizing the purchase of blankets, sponge mattresses, clothes and more food. As I prepared to leave in the Land-Rover on a run for supplies, I noticed a young man wandering aimlessly around the churchyard.

'*Hej ti*,' I called out. 'We're driving to Korçë. Why don't you come with us?' A little light rose in his face and he nodded.

'*Si e ke emrin*?' I asked.

'Ali,' he replied.

As we left the outskirts of Ersekë, Ali's tears began. In a low voice he started to recount the horrors he had seen as he left his country. Along with other members of his village, he had been ordered by Serbian paramilitaries to line up facing a wall. He had heard the blasting of a machine-gun behind him and the groans and screams of the people he knew.

'I closed my eyes. I knew that I was going to die,' he sobbed. 'Then the bullets stopped. I looked to my left and two men next to me were standing. Beyond those the people were on the floor. The men shouted at us to get out. The gun had no more bullets. We left them there by the wall …'

We were all silent. I sat watching the roadside fence posts passing by the windows of the car. Ali's was the first testimony that I had heard at close hand, and I was deeply distressed by it. Tero tried to reassure Ali of God's presence, and I held on to him as he shook. He had not been able to show his tears before his family. Apart from his grandfather, he was the only male with them and they were now his responsibility.

On our return from Korçë we left Ali to wander back into the overcrowded church building. As we unloaded blankets and toiletries into the church for distribution, a realization came over me. With the resources we had, the church could take care of some of the refugees for perhaps several days, but beyond that what would we do with them? How were we going to look after them? We were willing, but the needs were way beyond our means.

As I watched the TV news broadcasts later that day, the breaking story was of a potential disaster on the border of Macedonia and Kosova. Sixty thousand refugees were massing in open fields north of Skopje at a place called Blace, having fled the escalating conflict. The rain was pouring down on them as they huddled under pieces of plastic sheeting for shelter. The Macedonians were refusing to let them enter, the Serbs were refusing to let them back in, and they were trapped between them in no-man's-land. Everyone in the town was talking about it.

Over the next few days, the believers and the people of Ersekë began to give what they could, but few people had large reserves beyond what they needed themselves. The children at the school turned up with biscuits, bread and eggs they'd gathered; one boy in the church talked his father into slaughtering a sheep to donate; Xhani, Bledi's mother, brought all the food that she had in the house. It all helped a little. Ersekë apartments were small and families large, with two or three people often sleeping in each room, so few refugees could be taken into homes. They remained in the church and the old kindergarten, and we cooked around the clock.

Around four days after the first refugees arrived, a further request came through to Beni the police chief from the Interior

Ministry. The Albanian government was considering taking in the refugees trapped at Blace on the Macedonian border, and they wanted an estimate of how many we could take in our town. As the red evening light shone across the apartment blocks and up through the walnut orchards to the flanks of Mount Gramoz, once again we scouted urgently around different locations. We confirmed our estimate of 2,500, and in a matter of hours word came back down from Tirana: the government was requesting that we organize transportation immediately to collect as many as the town could manage. Together with Tiku the mayor, we each pooled the funds that we had. Beni had already requisitioned a number of minibus-taxis in preparation; some town drivers offered their services free, and those who couldn't afford to make the run were helped with the money they needed for diesel. Later that evening, a convoy of ten minibus-taxis and a coach left Ersekë to drive through the night to Macedonia.

And so it was that the huge exodus of the refugees trapped at Blace began, initially with a Dunkirk-like spirit as many towns in the southeast of Albania joined in with convoys, until the Macedonians themselves laid on their own transport to ship out the Kosovars. The football stadium in Korçë, where we had held our campaign, was used as the staging post as over twenty thousand people flooded in for distribution around the country. I remember the cold, clear air the next morning as I looked out over the stadium grass heaving with a mass of displaced people. The scene was strangely quiet as families huddled together in a stunned state of bewilderment and exhaustion. Occasionally, someone cried out hysterically as the traumas that had befallen them became too heavy to contain. From Korçë stadium, 2,500 were brought within hours over Qafë e Qarrit to the football stadium in Ersekë. From there we led them en masse to the locations we had chosen: the old kindergarten, the new one we had been renovating, the school dormitory, and an old wood factory on the edge of the town. Suddenly, the influx was upon us. Throughout it all, I was running on a surge of adrenaline to help them, but I felt heavy with their tremendous sorrow.

Of the 2,500 refugees who arrived in Ersekë, the number falling under our care grew rapidly as the town struggled to cope with the influx. We poured all the funds we had into the crisis; a Dutch Christian development agency with offices in the town gave us an extra donation, and we took collections from the believers. It was all swallowed up within days, however, as Caralee, Mark's wife Ruth, Xhani and many others cooked in marathon shifts and we attempted to clothe and provide bedding for everyone.

Many in the church began to spend hours wandering around the buildings listening to the Kosovars and trying to comfort them. Every refugee had a story that they needed to tell. There was such overwhelming sorrow and pain.

As I made my way about the school dormitory one evening, I came across a heavily pregnant woman with chestnut hair and striking features. She had been trying to sleep at nights on a single foam mattress with her husband, three children and her sister. There was no space remaining in any of the rooms, so all of them were relegated to the cold, institutional corridor. As I chatted with her and her husband, I learnt a little of their story; it was typical of the Blace refugees. While NATO bombs illuminated the night sky of Pristina, Metija and her family had been evicted from their home at gunpoint by Serbian police. She had been allowed no time to contact her parents as the Serbs forced them along to the railway station with other Albanians being ethnically cleansed. Some people had died there in the cold; some mothers had given birth as they waited on the platforms. Eventually they had been herded with hundreds of others on to a packed Macedonia-bound train. At points on the journey the train had been stopped and the men separated from the women, but whatever was being instigated that day was not carried through, and eventually they were all allowed back to their relatives. At the border with Macedonia, Metija had waited with her family in an open field as the days dragged on and the rain turned it into mud. They had had neither food nor shelter there, and she almost froze. At the end of the seventh day, they were transported out, not knowing where they were being taken. Thousands of others, however, had been marched back into Kosova to an uncertain fate. Now here she was, on a cold corridor floor in Ersekë. She did not know whether her parents were still alive, and she was deeply depressed about the future. She did not think that the Serbs or Slobodan Milosevic would ever leave Kosova, or that she would ever be able to return home. And she was ill, as well. I arranged for the family to be housed at the church in better conditions, and Caralee kept an eye on Metija's needs.

One afternoon in the cluttered office of our little publishing house, now stacked up with bales of blankets, carrier bags full of underwear and medical supplies, we cried out to the Lord to help us as the realities of the situation pressed in. I was tearing my hair out over all the problems and difficulties that needed to be solved every day. Others were crying with the scale of the suffering and the burden of care we felt under. We were just days away from a financial crisis: no aid from the international donors had reached Ersekë to help us, and what had arrived in Albania was being consumed by the overwhelming needs in Tirana and the refugee camps in the north. Every day now there was talk of more arrivals in Ersekë.

'Lord,' I implored, 'you are taking us one step further than we want to go! You are challenging us to go forward, and we are, but we can't keep doing it! What are we supposed to do with all these people?' I held my head in my hands as others continued to pray.

Early one evening that week, I received a telephone call from a man who introduced himself as Rob Frost, a pastor in England. This was miracle enough: connections into the country varied from erratic to virtually impossible. He explained that a Methodist conference known as the Easter People, with which he was involved, was about to gather in the town of Bournemouth in a few days' time.

'We'd like to do something to help the refugees if we can,' he said. His offer was more than welcome. A live telephone link-up to their Easter service was suggested: when the hour came, I held the receiver firmly but struggled to contain my emotions as I explained to the delegates the condition of the Kosovars and the crisis we were facing in Ersekë. The resulting collection raised a huge amount of money. Working together with Christ The Rock, a Bristol church which had always supported us, within three days they had dispatched two full truckloads of aid direct to us.

At this time I had no idea how the Easter People knew of our existence. I was later to discover that an old lady who had been praying for our work for years had found herself in a queue with Rob Frost, and presented him with a brief report. God had used her, Rob and Christ The Rock wondrously. When the trucks arrived they had precisely what was needed: blankets, beds, clothing, toiletries and basic foodstuffs. Christ The Rock also flew out two shipments of camp beds to Thessaloniki, and others helped transport them to the border. We had so desperately needed bedding: many of the old and sick were still sleeping on stone floors. We had felt that we were drowning under a human tide, but the aid deliveries lifted everyone's faith tremendously. As Caralee and Mark wrote reports about the Kosovars and e-mailed them to the UK and the US, further support began to gather.

Throughout the month of April, the number of refugees coming under our care at the church continued to grow. We had people with both the heart to get involved and the ability to organize and lead, and we eventually took over complete care of around 1,400 Kosovars, challenging them to get involved in taking care of themselves. Donations from individuals and churches in the West Country, New Jersey and California began to pour in, and many individuals made their way down to Ersekë to help us in whatever way they could. I had been aware of a 'fishing net' of relationships stretching across the world that had been woven over our years in Albania, and of our inter-dependency in it. Now this whole Body of Christ pulled together in support as never before, and I felt deeply strengthened and humbled by what was happening.

Despite all the sudden new pressures, we kept up our regular services at the church building, and a group of around thirty Kosovars, touched by the friendships they had formed, began to come along to our meetings. We learnt that much of the Kosovars' anger could be directed at the cross. It had often been used as a terrorizing symbol by the Serbs in the way that the Nazis had used the swastika. Streets and doors in Kosova had been marked with the cross as a warning that the people would soon be 'visited'. To them, 'our God' represented part of the reason they were here. The services were often highly charged and emotional events for everyone, but one occasion stands out above all the rest: a young Ersekë boy stepped forward to pray, and poured out his heart to God for the Kosovars with an uninhibited simplicity that children alone are capable of. As I opened my eyes and looked around, almost everyone in the room was weeping. No one could even say 'Amen': we were all at a loss for words.

The refugees, up to fifty in a room, spent day after day simply waiting, dozing on foam mattresses, smoking Cooper and

Assos cigarettes or toasting green peppers on tiny electric stoves. As I went round visiting them, I felt a deep need to offer them some hope. 'Lord,' I prayed, 'what can I say to them? How can I lift their spirits?'

Often we would chat about Tony Blair and the effects of the NATO bombing campaign, and I would ask whether they had heard any news of lost relatives. The question that everyone wanted answered, however, was when they would be going home. There was no end in sight to the conflict, but somehow I felt confident enough to say: 'You will all be home by the fourth of July. The war will be over, and it will be independence for you!' It might have been foolish, but it spread a little optimism. Everyone knew, though, that this was a question only God could answer.

Early in May, NATO troops began to move into the Korçë area. A vast temporary city was erected south of the town on the road to Qafë e Qarrit. Both AFOR and KFOR set up their bases and began erecting long rows of canvas tents in readiness. The word was that thousands more Kosovars were to be brought into the area, and NATO was scouting everywhere for locations to set up camps. A French major and two junior officers soon visited us at the church and asked us to guide them around the land outside Ersekë. We helped them as best we could, but my French was as poor as their English, and as they left I half-jokingly prayed: 'Lord, if we have to work with NATO, let it be someone I can communicate with!'

The following day, I set off in the Land-Rover on an errand to Korçë with Mondi, my driver, and a couple of the refugees. As we rounded a bend in the road at the top of Qafë e Qarrit, I noticed a long line of Land-Rovers, each with bright orange circles on top, heading towards us along the flank of the mountain. As we turned another bend, we realized that the vehicles had deliberately blocked the way. They belonged to the British army. Mondi braked and I stepped down into the road. The officer in charge jumped down from his vehicle and strode over to introduce himself.

'Brigadier Tim Cross. Nice to see you. I was coming to meet you, actually! Taking some of my boys down to Ersekë. Would you mind going back?' he began, in swift, short sentences.

'Er ... no,' I replied, taken aback.

'Would you mind if I get in your car?' he continued.

I gestured for him to do so, and Mondi turned the vehicle around. The Brigadier sat in the rear in his camouflage uniform and green beret and I sat in the front. Mondi had been a driver in the Albanian military and had chauffeured many senior officers before, but we were now the lead vehicle in a convoy of six Land-Rovers and I could sense his pleasure.

'He's sitting behind you. People will think that you outrank him!' he whispered with a smirk.

'So what are you doing down here?' the Brigadier enquired. I was considering how best to reply when he remarked, 'Bit of a preacher myself!'

All along the road back to Ersekë we continued to talk. I explained a little about our work in Albania and about the Kosovars in our town, and in the course of conversation it transpired that Brigadier General Cross was a lay-reader in the Anglican Church! As the senior NATO officer for the area, his brief was to prepare camps for refugees from the north of Albania, to relieve the strain and to clear the front line if KFOR entered Kosova in a ground war. He explained that he was looking to establish sites for fifty thousand people. My heart almost skipped a beat.

At the church building we gave Brigadier Cross a cup of tea. To everyone's satisfaction, he explained that he'd heard reports from his monitors that the church in Ersekë was running 'a good operation', and that he'd wanted to see it himself. I introduced him to the town leaders, Tiku and Beni, and we all scouted west of the town for possible locations. Within an hour, Brigadier Cross had selected a site and proposed British soldiers build a camp there, with its management to be placed under our charge. It was difficult to comprehend it all – but I had prayed for someone I could communicate with! Our leaders were all growing daily, forged in a fire of sheer necessity, but we were willing to take on the challenge. I shook hands with the Brigadier, and he and his officers left for the NATO base in Korçë.

A few days after the meeting, a fleet of Chinook helicopters began dropping tents close to the pinewoods. The tremendous whirr of their twin propeller blades drew huge crowds out from the town. Within two weeks, the site was prepared for a further four thousand refugees, with row after row of white canvas tents flapping in readiness in the spring breeze. We approached World Relief, an American Christian relief and development agency, to partner us in running the camp, and continued to plan and make preparations for the arrival of more Kosovars.

It was an unimaginable series of developments. At the start of the crisis I had felt that we might care for around thirty refugees: now six thousand was not looking impossible. We had all felt under incredible pressure, though, and now that stress increased. There was so much that needed to be done every day, and we could take no time off. I was often working from around six in the morning through to late in the evening, when I collapsed on the bed exhausted. If I remained stationary for more than half an hour, my brain seemed to close itself down like a dysfunctional piece of software. Late one afternoon, as I left the town hall, I blacked out on the steps into the square. I came round to find Mondi and Tiku leaning over me and helping me up.

Brigadier Cross kept in regular contact and we had further opportunities to discuss Albanian culture and issues of how relationships work in the country. The Brigadier invited the leaders of the churches within our movement to a private meeting at the NATO base south of Korçë. There he laid on a special meal and delivered a talk he had prepared for them on leadership skills and the challenge of leading non-Christians. It was an inspiring talk from a man who, I had learned, was in charge of NATO logistics for the whole of the Kosova theatre. During the meeting, a UN official arrived to meet the Brigadier and was somewhat bemused as he sat in on our gathering. Brigadier Cross turned to me as he continued his address and winked.

'Of course,' he announced proudly, 'the greatest aid to my leadership has been my faith in Christ. To be a true leader, you need the Lord Jesus.' The UN official coughed, but from every-one else I sensed a hearty non-verbal 'Amen!' The Brigadier's gesture was an honour and a huge pat on the back to the entire church leadership. Everyone was being stretched beyond anything they had done before and beyond their level of com-petence. It was only by God's grace that things were holding together.

At a later point, a meeting was held at Cross's base for all the non-governmental organizations (NGOs) and others who were helping run the camps NATO had erected in the area. As well as those same church leaders, there were UN representa-tives, the local MP, the Prefect (a little like a regional governor) and many other officials. I felt a tremendous pride seeing Holger, Tero, Niko, Bledi and others being given equal respect for the part they were playing in caring for the refugees.

I once read a book by General Patton, one of America's top commanding officers in World War II, in which there was a statement about military life that has stayed with me ever since.

Soldiers, he said, become veterans not through the number of years they serve but through the battles they fight. Similarly, it seemed to me now that Christians took on spiritual maturity not through the number of years they had been believers but through the challenges and character battles they had overcome. As I looked around the table, I felt that, though they were all young in Christian years, they had every right to be there. I had been planning a challenge for them, a means of training for leadership, but God had had his own purposes for that.

The Prefect paid our church a visit one afternoon. As we talked together about the refugee crisis, he hugged me and paid the Albanian church real homage. 'I speak to other prefects around the country, Jani, and there are groups like yours holding Albania together,' he exclaimed, shaking his head. 'Your people are saving us here, and before the crisis we didn't even know you existed!'

Little evangelical communities had been stepping up to bat across the country: on the border at Kukes, running the huge refuge in Tirana's sports centre, and in many other towns. At a camp for 1,300 refugees at Lozhan, near Korçë, the situation had spun into anarchy. The government hadn't been able to control it; UNHCR had sent in their people and they had failed; but Holger and the church from Libonik took it over and ran it. The Prefect's comments felt like a tremendous validation, not of what we were involved in, but of what God was involved in across the country. The church in Ersekë was a piece of a much bigger work that God was putting together.

At the end of May, the whole landscape of our preparations for caring for the Kosovars pivoted 180 degrees on its axis. One fresh late spring afternoon, two Lynx helicopters hovered over Qafë e Qarrit and landed at the camp on the edge of Ersekë's pinewoods. Brigadier Cross was already visiting us at the site, and a further senior officer had flown in to visit him. At the church building, Brigadier Cross's visitor strode into the yard wearing a combat uniform and a cherry red beret with the Paras' emblem. His bearing announced that he was a man of considerable importance.

'Mike Jackson,' he announced with a quick shake of my hand. 'Good to meet you, my boy.'

We made a cup of tea for General Jackson, commander of KFOR on the ground, as he settled down to talk with Brigadier Cross in the office of our publishing house. Later, as he chatted a little with members of the church and smoked a large brown cigar, he made a comment that arrested me with its importance.

'NATO will be in Pristina one way or the other within the next two weeks,' he said in a gruff, almost grandfatherly voice. 'If it has to be by force, then the camps at Kukes and along the Macedonian border will be emptied.' Whatever was going to happen in the region, be that an influx or an exodus of Kosovars, was about to unfold.

That evening at the Korçë NATO base, Brigadier Cross described the situation to all those who were caring for refugees in the region, and explained that he was moving out in preparation.

'You know, Ian,' he said, as I got ready to return to Ersekë, 'it's a shame your people are not an NGO as such. Good organizations will quickly be needed by the Albanians inside Kosova.'

His remark struck a chord with me. I talked it over with the church leadership that night and telephoned him back. 'When the time comes, I think we might be able to put together a team to work with our returning Kosovars,' I explained. I had already begun to think as far ahead as I could manage.

It was during the first week of June, after 72 days of aerial bombardment, that Slobodan Milosevic finally backed down and agreed to meet all NATO's demands. The Serbs began to pull their military vehicles back up the highway to Belgrade, and still the villages in Kosova could be seen burning as they left. At dawn on Saturday 12 June, General Jackson's troops swept into Kosova, clearing the highway to the capital of lethal anti-personnel mines. Seventy-two hours after the first troops hit the ground in Pristina, we received a telephone call from Brigadier Cross's staff, informing us that it would be safe for us to enter if we wished.

I set off immediately in the Land-Rover with Mark and some staff from World Relief. During the long journey along the shore of Lake Pogradec, up into Macedonia and north through the country to Blace, I wondered what we would see inside Kosova. I had been asking myself what responsibilities we had to the Kosovars who had fallen under our care. Now that the war was over, did we just send them back to what remained of their homes with a tidy aid parcel? We had become committed to them as friends: what would a true friend do? I felt touched by the message of the book of Nehemiah. He had rebuilt the walls of Jerusalem, and with them the spirit of the nation for the returning Jewish exiles. Perhaps now, with the Lord's help, we might rebuild a small piece of Kosova for the refugees in Ersekë.

North of Blace, we joined the main highway to Pristina. There, thousands of Kosovars had begun flooding back into the land in KFOR's wake. Along with the returning refugees, convoys of dark green military vehicles – tankers, armoured personnel carriers and Land-Rovers – vied for the road with taxis laden with TV crews and journalists. Overhead was the heavy drone of helicopter traffic. Ethnic Albanians were returning home on every conceivable form of transport. Cars were piled high, with luggage strapped to the roof and bulging out of boots. Donkeys and tiny tractors pulled along wooden hay carts teetering to the point of collapse with carpets, refrigerators and families, all packed together under plastic sheeting. All along the roadside, roofless houses stared with blackened facades, and the sky was darkened with smoke. Children flashed us the victory sign from carts and steamed-up car windows as we passed. Blood-red Albanian flags with the black eagle flew rippling in the wind. Car horns were sounding in victory celebration and frustration: everyone wanted to get back home as fast as they were able. It reminded me of pictures I'd seen of the liberation of Paris at the end of the Second World War, and the feeling of euphoria was infectious.

In the town of Gjakove the devastation we saw was horrifying. Using their tanks and artillery, the Serbs had 'scorched the earth'. House after house had been flattened to rubble, with masonry and roof beams strewn into the road. There were buckled lamp-posts, smashed trees and upturned and burned-out car shells, and the minaret of the mosque lay decapitated on top of its dome. We saw people wandering, gaunt and emaciated, having emerged from months of hiding in cellars and nearby forests. As we walked around, I came across a young girl in a dirty yellow dress. 'Freedom! Freedom!' she cried, as I talked a little with her father. It was all deeply affecting.

The buildings of the capital, Pristina, were far less damaged than we had expected. The city's politics had apparently been more moderate than the KLA's, so it had taken less of a punishment. The TV tower, however, had been struck by a NATO missile that had frazzled its roof into a twisted mesh of metal and blown out its windows. Looting had also been widespread. Challenger tanks were patrolling everywhere, and British paratroopers in their cherry-red berets were positioned on most street corners, clutching their machine-guns. Occasionally, the crack of sniper fire made us flinch; KFOR were still clearing houses as rogue Serbs took pot shots at returning Albanians.

Movement around Pristina was strictly controlled, and we had been given a password – 'sunrise' – which gave us a degree of freedom. We found a location we could use as a base, and as we talked over how our mission to Kosova might develop, we changed the word 'sunrise' to 'Son-rise'. Maybe now, we thought, it was time for the Son of God to rise over Kosova.

When our party arrived back in Ersekë, four days after we had left, we were deluged with questions about what we had seen. Everyone wanted to know what Kosova was like. 'Have you seen my village, my house?' people beseeched us. The terrible reality was that many had neither to return to. Now the burning question was, when could they go back? After four or more months in exile, they were desperate to get home. NATO was saying that Pristina was fine, but the UN was discouraging anyone from going home yet. Those refugees who had any resources of their own, however, immediately began jumping on to buses and taxis for Tirana, and then on to Kukes and the border.

I appealed at the church for believers who felt called to return with the Kosovars to let the leadership know, and we were overwhelmed with those who were ready. More were willing than there were opportunities for service, and it was hard for many who had formed close bonds with the Kosovars to feel that their tasks were coming to an end.

Niko led a small advance team to Pristina. The first phase of their brief was to carry out a damage assessment of all our refugees' homes. How many of them were left standing? How could we now help?

As the days of June moved on, we began to help the Ersekë refugees return home. We found coach drivers who were prepared to make the journey to Kosova after we reassured them that we could get them through NATO checkpoints. With some of the money that churches around the world had sent us, we were able to pay for them and their diesel, and soon we had an Ersekë–Pristina shuttle service running. During these days, we shared the Kosovars' joy at returning, now heavily laden – aid from the international community had finally arrived in the last two weeks.

I remember the strong handshakes and the bloodshot eyes of both the Muslim Kosovars and the Ersekë Christians. Our relationship with them had strained to breaking point at times, but right now we felt the warmth of their gratitude. Many Kosovars remembered the words I'd shared about them being home before the fourth of July: by God's grace, it was coming to pass. I watched one particular packed bus rock along the pot-holed road from the church building, back along the route down which the first bus had arrived. I remembered the old man with the little white fez who Beni and I had coaxed off that coach twelve weeks earlier. Now Meti, a young boy with cup-handle ears and a precocious grin, was pressing his face against the glass and waving, and I felt my eyes begin to prick.

The kindergartens and school dormitory soon seemed strangely empty: mattresses and blankets lay crumpled on the floor, the odd bag of green peppers was left sitting on a table. By early July, only one family remained living at the church building. Metija, the pregnant woman with chestnut hair from Pristina, was now to be seen smiling and lighter in her expression; she had often prayed with Caralee. The birth of all her other children had been long and painful, but on 6 July at the town hospital she bore a baby girl with swift ease. She knew that this was God's special favour to her, and we all shared in her happiness.

The town, too, was quiet. Niko was now heading up our team in Pristina, and fourteen believers including Angela, Bledi and Elisi (Caralee's other 'bodyguard') eventually joined him there, as well as workers from World Relief. Over the summer months, they completed a damage assessment programme covering over a thousand homes in Pristina, Ostrazub, Peja,

Fushë Kosova and Malisheva, from where our refugees had fled. Ninety per cent of their properties had been looted, and 55 per cent had been destroyed. We recruited a team of forty craftsmen in Ersekë – men who were not believers but who were willing to come under Niko's leadership. Five years earlier, such an arrangement would have been unimaginable: now he and others commanded respect in the town. I continued to make journeys into Kosova to monitor the progress of our work, but Niko was running the whole operation. Before the winter months set in, the team had rebuilt over 130 homes.

If the conditions they had to work in were hard, it was harder still for the returning Kosovars, living in tents or the burnt shells of their homes without water or electricity supplies. The Serbs had also left mines everywhere, but thanks to his military service Niko was skilled in their removal, and he was able to clear houses before work began.

The team had to face many horrors along with the refugees, sometimes removing the bodies of loved ones left where they'd been slaughtered. Often, though, the trauma was the discovery of a treasured home looted and burnt. I remember accompanying Mark and a man with coal-black hair and a thin, salesman's moustache along the dirt road to his house in Fush Kosova. As we rounded a stone wall, he saw his truck; it was just where he had left it, but now it was a blackened, rusting shell. His house had sooty flame marks rising like tongues above the windows, and the roof had collapsed into the interior. He did not have to hide his feelings, as his family were not with us, and he broke down and wept. Mark hugged him until he recovered a little. 'The only thing that keeps me going,' he told us later, 'is knowing that it was me that made that house, and not that house that made me.' His courage was admirable.

One weather-beaten old man in the shattered town of Peja told me that as the team helped him rebuild his home he had seen 'true Christianity'. I like to think that, in the eyes of the Muslim Kosovars who met the believers in Ersekë, there had been some redemption of the name 'Christian' from the abuse it had suffered from the Serbian militia.

Though we saw a small number of the refugees come to faith in Christ, it was a moment of especially deep thankfulness for me when I heard news of young Meti with the cup-handle ears: we had all been praying for him. From the earliest days of his arrival in Ersekë, Meti had demanded attention with a cheekiness that won everyone's heart. He would sneak in on leadership meetings at the church, proudly sitting upright as the only refugee present, and grinning as he was treated equally to a cup of tea and a biscuit. When General Jackson had flown down in his Lynx helicopter to meet Brigadier Cross, Meti had gate-crashed that meeting, too.

But the most famous occasion was one afternoon in Ersekë, when the Democratic Party had organized a meeting to rally the refugees to their affiliated party back home in Kosova. The one-time president of Albania, Sali Berisha, arrived at the kindergarten we were renovating, where around two hundred Kosovars were living. Crowds had gathered to hear his address. The dignitaries stood shaking each other's hands while a huddle of bodyguards surrounded the man in sunglasses, anxiously keeping watch all around. As Sali stood in his smart suit, waving the two-fingered Democrats' gesture as he spoke, Meti pushed his way through the crowd. He side-stepped one bodyguard, ducked through the legs of another and then walked boldly up to the politician and tugged on his trouser leg.

'I am Meti,' he announced proudly, 'and who might you be?'

The little boy was showered with sweets and biscuits for weeks afterwards by the town Socialists, who always spun the story that, like Meti, no one knew who Sali Berisha was any more. In fairness to the politician, however, he had given Meti ten Deutschmarks, and Meti was proud of that.

Though we were not fully aware of it at the time, Meti and his brother had lost their father, grandfather and all their close male relatives in the Kosova tragedy. When the team from our church had arrived at the blackened shell of Meti's home, the bodies of some of them were found dumped in the garden well.

As the year drew to a close, it was Angela who told me, as she and Bledi remained in Kosova to work with widows from the war, that Meti had discovered his Heavenly Father. We continue to pray for him, and for many others in Kosova.

EPILOGUE

Workers from the church in Ersekë remained in Kosova helping widows from the conflict until May of the following year.
The workers organized the buying of cows and chickens for
many families to help them back along the road to self-suffi-
ciency. In Ersekë, the old grain stores prepared as winter hous-
ing for the refugees were converted into a base for Christian
camps and retreats all year round, and north in Libonik the
believers planted two more embryonic churches over the summer months.

During the year 2000, it became increasingly obvious that
the church in Ersekë had grown to the point where it no longer
needed Ian and Caralee's leadership and would continue to be
effective without them. The time had come once more for
them to move on. In talking with the increasing number of
Albanian leaders in the southeast of the country, it had become
clear that God was redirecting them back to Korçë – to the
town where their work had begun. There they are preparing to
foster the development of more of the Christian leaders who
are in such great demand.

Only nine years earlier there had been just a handful of
Albanian Protestant Christians in the entire country. Now
there are several thousand throughout. Where there was once
one bible study group in Korçë, there are now ten fledgling

churches and many other bible study groups. May the freedom and new life that are rooted in the gospel continue to touch the people of Albania.

CONTACT DETAILS

Anyone wishing to find out more about the current ministry of Ian and Caralee in Albania can contact them at oacialbania@aol.com or at OAC Albania, c/o 18 St Hilary Close, Stoke Bishop, Bristol, BS9 1DA, United Kingdom.